MICROGREENS

MICROGREENS
A GUIDE TO GROWING NUTRIENT-PACKED GREENS

Eric Franks and Jasmine Richardson

Photographs by Margaux Gibbons

GIBBS SMITH
TO ENRICH AND INSPIRE HUMANKIND
Salt Lake City | Charleston | Santa Fe | Santa Barbara

First Edition
13 12 11 10 09   5 4 3 2

Text © 2009 Eric Franks and Jasmine Richardson
Photographs © 2009 Margaux Gibbons except the following:
Sara Remington, pages 8, 44, 52, 62, 65, 162
Jasmine Richardson, page 26
Craig Lovell, page 27
Ariel Williams (sketch), pages 123, 124

Published by
Gibbs Smith
P.O. Box 667
Layton, Utah 84041

Orders: 1.800.835.4993
www.gibbs-smith.com

Designed by fusionmarketing.com
Printed and bound in China
Gibbs Smith books are printed on either recycled, 100% post-consumer waste, or FSC-certified papers or on paper
produced from a 100% certified sustainable forest / controlled wood source.

Library of Congress Cataloging-in-Publication Data

Franks, Eric, 1978-
  Microgreens / Eric Franks and Jasmine Richardson; photographs by Margaux Gibbons. — 1st ed.
    p. cm.
  ISBN-13: 978-1-4236-0364-1
  ISBN-10: 1-4236-0364-8
  1. Greens, Edible. 2. Cookery (Greens) I. Richardson, Jasmine. II. Title.
  SB339.F73 2009
  635'.5—dc22
                          2008030670

To our son, Haven

He is the light of our lives and represents a bright future for this world. He came into our lives while writing this book and has expanded our hearts beyond belief.

We also dedicate this book to all of the farmers that have taken the time to share their wisdom so that the craft of traditional farming can continue and flourish. Thank you to Tim and Fabienne Rapsey, Eliot Coleman, Barbara Damrosch, Siri Beringer, Paul Birdsall, and all of the other fine people who have helped us along the way.

A special thanks to Jennifer Gillespie for the guidance and inspiration she has given us over the years.

Lastly, we have newfound gratitude for our parents as we start our journey with Haven. Our lives would not be possible without the love and support that they have given us.

Thank you.

CONTENTS

9 Foreword

11 Introduction

15 Why Microgreens?

25 Health and Microgreens

33 Materials

45 How-to-Grow Ten-Step Process

63 Individual Crops

115 Composting

129 Recipes: Food as Art

169 Troubleshooting

177 Recommended Books and Resources

185 Sources

190 Index

FOREWORD

Over the years, quite a number of young people have worked with us here on the farm. They arrive bright-eyed and eager to learn more about farming and we try not to disappoint that expectation. Over the course of all four seasons, they help us to produce and market some 35 different vegetable crops plus numerous fruits, herbs, and flowers. When they depart after a year or two, they scatter to the corners of the earth, some to pursue new, untried interests, but many to carve out a career in the broad world of food production. Jasmine and Eric are members of the latter brigade. They were great workers and became staunch friends. It gives us great joy to see them taking their place in the ever-growing ranks of small-scale, earth-friendly farmers. And we heartily celebrate their skill and expertise in the production of that most exquisite of salad ingredients—microgreens.

From the moment a seed sprouts, new life and new life giving forces are being created. The quality of the soil and the care of the grower are the guiding hands. At every step in its life cycle the plant offers different culinary possibilities to the imaginative cook, possibilities that are becoming increasingly recognized in kitchens everywhere. It takes a great deal of knowledge of soils and irrigation and attention to detail to nurture those seeds to the desired stage of growth, and then much careful thinking and planning to harvest, pack, and market them at a sufficient profit to make your living farming. Three cheers to Jasmine and Eric for their success in pursuing this goal and then presenting it so clearly and thoroughly in this book for others to follow, both farmers and home gardeners alike. Bon appetit!

—Eliot Coleman and Barbara Damrosch
Harborside, Maine

INTRODUCTION

We met on a small farm in rural Pennsylvania. Linked by our love for food and small-scale agriculture, we traveled the country working on diversified farms. We studied market gardening, farming with draft horses, sustainable animal husbandry, and intensive four-season greenhouse production.

During our travels and training, we learned about microgreens. We began growing them in the dead of winter at Barbara Damrosch's and Eliot Coleman's Four Season Farm on the tip of Cape Rosier in Harborside, Maine. One of the philosophies behind their farm was "farming on the backside of the calendar," so we suited up in our long johns for a long Maine winter. While we focused on the winter salad production, we also experimented with growing microgreens as something new and different to offer our local chefs. As the season progressed and spring set in, the responsibilities of the farm took us away from this niche. Looking back, it seemed as if this short stint would be the only time that we would grow these little beauties.

After we left the farm, we peeled off the long johns and moved to coastal California, beginning the search for land to start our own farm. We moved to Big Sur, where we had family and friends, and although beautiful, it is not the ideal place to find farmland. However, it served as the perfect home base for starting our hunt. We found a place to rent on the side of a mountain with less than one hundredth of an acre of flat ground. At first sight it didn't look like a good place to grow anything, and by now we had been away from life on the farm for several months. We missed getting our hands in the earth. Remembering the small amount of space microgreens required, we started a few trays for ourselves on our porch.

Slowly, we began bringing samples down to local restaurants. As demand grew, we grew with it. Our porch quickly went from a place to sit and relax in the sun to a greens-growing haven. Suddenly, we found ourselves spending all of our free time honing and refining our new craft. We experimented with different varieties, exploring the never-ending variation in flavor and appearance while catering to the local chefs. We did many trials on soil, seed, and water pH to learn what each crop preferred. We became fully immersed in the world of microgreens.

Struck by their nutritional potency, we started thinking of the difference they could make not only in our community but in others as well. We loved the beauty they brought to the dishes created by chefs but wished we could get these greens to the broader public and in larger quantities. Without requiring a large financial investment or substantial previous knowledge, microgreens could provide a stepping-stone on the path to nutritional independence. Communities around the world could easily nourish themselves while enriching the land around them, adding fertility for future generations.

As we shared the health benefits of microgreens and their accessibility with others, we were surprised by the universal excitement everyone felt about them. Growing their own microgreens seemed like something they could easily do and even enjoy. We worked on simplifying our system so that we could share this knowledge with even more people.

A common limitation many face when trying to grow their own food is the commitment it requires to take on a garden. Just as spring and summer are the busiest times of the garden, they are also busy times in people's lives. We are often taken away from our homes during the summer months, leaving a well-intentioned garden as a burden or forgotten responsibility. Home gardens are often filled with beautiful produce with no one but the birds to eat it. Growing your own microgreens allows you to stop and start whenever you want, leaving you with less of a commitment to attend to—thus allowing more time, flexibility, and ease for your life.

The purpose of *Microgreens* is to give you an avenue to the joy of growing and eating your own food. We can imagine a time when every rooftop, windowsill, and small yard is alive with trays of microgreens. Even people driving campers across the country could be growing a tray in their window while germinating another under the bed. You will find that growing greens is surprisingly easy. We will show you each of the simple steps it takes to grow, harvest, and prepare your own microgreens.

WHY MICROGREENS?

Over the past twenty years, interest in local, fresh, and organic food has been on the rise. There has been a rejuvenation of the small farm and a renewal of appreciation for fresh vegetables. The revival of the farmers market, the inception of the CSA model (Community Supported Agriculture), and the overall movement towards clean, whole foods has been extraordinary and is continuing to grow. People are rediscovering the importance of fresh, locally grown food. This movement has shown that it is not just for the affluent, not only for those interested in farming, but for the whole of the population and future generations.

With their ability to accentuate and deepen our connection with nature, we believe that microgreens have a place in the growing interest of food. Harvested very early in their lives, microgreens are tender, delicate, and highly flavorful. They have a crisp yet melt-in-your-mouth texture and a variety of flavors that swing from sweet to savory to earthy to spicy. Throw in the exuberant beauty of their reds, yellows, greens, and purples and you have a salad that is pure delight. With all of the varied tastes and textures, integrating microgreens into your diet can be fun and easy. Embarking on this venture of growing and eating your own greens doesn't require that you change your diet. Packed with great taste, these little greens can be added to just about anything. Eaten alone as a salad or added to soups, entrées, sandwiches, burgers, or anything else you can imagine, microgreens will enhance your food and your life.

Over the past few years, microgreens have gained popularity as a hot new culinary trend. From New York to Los Angeles, chefs have been enjoying them as a way to creatively accentuate plates of food and add new depths of flavor to their dishes. While this trend has grown, a select few growers have taken advantage of this niche market. Even in metropolitan hubs, where chefs are able to buy most of their produce from farmers markets, much of the microgreens market has been dominated by mail order.

For the Commercial Grower

Growing microgreens is a way of expanding the scope of your operation to include this largely untapped market. We have never shown our greens to a chef who wasn't excited about using them. This excitement is filtering into the consumer market as well, making demand even stronger. As more and more people are experiencing the qualitative difference of fresh local produce, your microgreens will sell easily. Offering your community this year-round resource can be a great way to diversify your operation. Another benefit these greens offer is their ability to bring in quick farm income while also contributing to its fertility.

On many farms it often takes at least a couple of months to start recouping the money invested in potting soils and composts. While the small farm's primary focus is not usually

on making a buck but rather the health of the land and its surrounding community, steady income is essential to meeting the needs of the farm and farm family.

Microgreens require minimal initial investment, with most varieties costing less than two dollars per tray for seed and soil. Once sown, they can start generating income in just two to three weeks.

After your trays have been harvested, composting your soil now filled with stem and root matter is also quick and easy. In the heat of the summer this soil can be amended, composted, and ready to use in under a month. We have made a special worm bin for this purpose. As our trays are composted, a large amount of earthworm castings are added to the soil, enriching it even further. At this point it can be used to start your seedlings, incorporated into your fields, or even used to grow more microgreens. With all of their advantages, you can see why microgreens can enhance the small farm.

For the Home Grower

Growing your own microgreens gives you access to fresh, living greens all year long with minimal investment of money, time, or previous knowledge. The little amount of space they require makes them a perfect fit for both urban and suburban families who do not have room for a garden. Suddenly we are given the opportunity to create masterpieces in our own kitchens. You will see how microgreens can transcend the gourmet world and become part of everyday life. They give us an opportunity to slow down and appreciate the beauty of food. Taking the time to experience our food in this way is a wonderful gift to give to ourselves and our families.

Aside from their extraordinary taste and aesthetic appeal, microgreens are also extremely nutritious. The ability to harvest and eat them within minutes gives you access to their most nutritionally rich state. They give us a strong dose of digestible vitamins, minerals, and phytonutrients. While your taste buds enjoy their intense flavor, your body will reap the benefits of their concentrated nutrients.

It's a rare thing to eat something so good that you get goose bumps from how delicious and alive it is. We have been growing and eating microgreen salads for years and still the very thought of fixing one for ourselves puts smiles on our faces. We are always amazed at how much we can eat in one sitting; it's comparable to drinking a cold glass of water on a hot summer's day. Your body is in complete agreement with your mind that this, right now, is the greatest thing you could give yourself.

Children and Microgreens

Growing microgreens is not just for adults! It can be a fun and easy way for children to connect with nature. Microgreens provide an engaging project at home or at school, teaching about where food comes from and how to grow it. Children have more of a connection to things if they are a part of the process. Seeds become their seeds that grow into their greens. An identity and connection is formed with the plants and their progress. Molly Katzen described this phenomenon when she talked about taking a group of school kids to "The Pizza Farm" in northern California. The kids spent time watching and learning about all of the components that made up pizza; the cows that produced the milk that made the cheese, the fields that grew the wheat that they ground into flour to make the crust, and the growing herbs and tomatoes that made up the sauce. Then, they made their own pizza. She

described the anticipation as they waited for their pizza to finish baking; each one checking every couple of minutes to see if their masterpieces were complete. This excitement doesn't happen while our little ones wait for frozen pizza to appear on their plates. It is a gift to give our children an awareness of their food and its process. Especially in suburban and urban areas, many children today aren't quite sure where food comes from. If one has never seen a carrot harvested out of the earth, how would you know that is where it came from? It could be just as logical that a carrot comes from a can or simply from the store. Starting microgreens with your children gives them a chance to get their hands in the earth. It gives them the opportunity to discover what else is growing in the soil. It becomes alive in their minds, as

they watch worms break down their kitchen scraps or seeds spring to life. You may even find your picky eaters asking for more greens on their dinner plates! Once this living world has been broached, the possibilities are endless. From a few simple seeds come brand-new eyes for nature.

Microgreens vs. Sprouts vs. Baby Greens

Sprouts, microgreens, and baby greens are all stages in a plant's development. Each has identifying characteristics and varying nutritional values. A sprout is the first stage of a seed's development. The word "sprout" is actually synonymous with germination. Grown in different types of containers, these seeds are kept moist and at room temperature until they germinate. Instead of allowing them to grow in a medium and establish into a plant, sprouts are consumed right after they germinate. Often slightly opaque and yielding a crunchy texture, they have become increasingly popular for their nutritional value.

When grown in a medium (soil or otherwise), the second stage of a seed's development involves the establishment of its roots and the opening of its first leaves, called cotyledons. Greens harvested at this stage are called microgreens. If microgreens are allowed to continue to grow, they put on their next set of leaves, called "true leaves." True leaves are the leaves of a plant that distinguish it from another plant. While many brassicas (cabbage, broccoli, arugula, etc.) all have very similar heart-shaped cotyledons, when their true leaves develop they look quite different and are easily distinguished from each other. These greens are harvested in their infancy, and are only allowed to grow in the soil for a week or two. They have all of the health benefits of sprouts with the added advantage of trace minerals brought up from the soil they are grown in. At this stage their texture, appearance, and flavor are much more like a salad green than a crunchy sprout. If the seed were allowed to continue to grow past the true leaf stage and, given enough space and time, it would eventually reach the baby green stage. Baby greens are tender leaves that are popular in salad mixes lled mesclun or spring mix. They are more flavorful and tender than leaves from a n head of lettuce but lose some of the intensity of flavor and nutritional value that at the microgreen stage.

Sprouts, microarugula, baby arugula

HEALTH
AND
MICROGREENS

Small diversified farm (Eliot Coleman and Barbara Damrosch's Four Season Farm, Harborside, ME)

As human beings, our roots lie in the soil. Although many of us have forgotten this important link over the past few generations, our connection with nature is so ancient and fundamental that it cannot be completely disregarded. If while we are eating we pause for a moment, we can easily follow our food back to the plants, the animals, the soil, and even the wind, rain, and sun. All of these things have their confluence on the farm. There is no avoiding that the health of the earth and the health of human beings are intimately tied.

Traditional agriculture has been practiced for thousands of years all over the world. Small scale and worked by hand, these farms are highly diversified and skillfully tended. Diversified farmers make the craft of soil stewardship their primary work, farming in a way that actually contributes to and enriches the life of the farm and everything and everyone that interacts with it. The animals raised here are alert with healthy coats. The soil is rich, dark, and sweet smelling. The plants are lush and grow vigorously with little sign of stress. The food grown here contributes balance and health to its surrounding community. Even the average passerby can notice that "inexplicable something" that permeates the air around such a farm.

The larger a farm is in scale and the larger its industrial intentions, the further it diverges from this diversified small-farm model. Over the last century there has been a gradual shift in the scale and focus of the farm in this country. By the end of World War II, it was commonly thought that modern, mechanized industrial systems were superior to small-scale traditional

Large scale monoculture (broccoli, Salinas Valley, CA)

methods. Along with industrialization came the beginning of chemical fertilizer use in agriculture. After the war, many of the compounds that were used in the production of bombs were transformed into agricultural fertilizers.

During this time, belief that farms needed to be large to take advantage of the factory philosophy took hold. Many farmers moved off the land and into the cities to join the growing trend of industry. The family farm slowly disappeared as big agri-business took hold.

Over the last century, the United States has lost over 4.5 million farms. According to the U.S. census bureau, the percentage of people living and working on farms has gone from 40 percent to less than 1 percent.

Along with this restructuring of our nation's farms came the inevitable compromise of the quality of produce available. In Paul Bergner's book, *The Healing Power of Minerals, Special Nutrients and Trace Elements,* USDA statistics are included that illustrate this decline. These figures show mineral and vitamin content declining in several types of fruits and vegetables between the years 1962 and 1992. Among others, calcium dropped by almost 30 percent, iron by 32 percent, and magnesium by 21 percent.

Produce nutrition is limited by the quality of soil it was grown in, how it was harvested, its treatment after harvest, and how old it is once it reaches your fork. To get a sense of how nutritious microgreens are, we must first look at how these variables affect the nutritional content of our produce.

Health and Soil

The interactions between plants and soil are so vast and complex that some people have dedicated their entire lives to study them. From these studies, scientists are reaffirming what the traditional farmer has known for thousands of years; diversity is one of the keys to healthy soil and therefore healthy plants and animals. Crop rotations, composts, soil amendments, sustainable animal husbandry, and the growing of a wide variety of vegetables all converge into the expanding diversity and fertility of the land. Produce grown in fertile ground is able

to acquire an abundance of phytonutrients, minerals, and trace elements. A focus on the health of soil biology leads to inherent pest and drought resistance, creating a farm that is able to sustain life indefinitely.

In conventional agriculture, soil has become merely a medium that holds our vegetables upright instead of the living, dynamic force that it should be. In this model, sustainable soil management is seen as in-efficient and inferior. Focus, instead, is put on large-scale single-crop production (mono-culture) and broad-spectrum chemical fertil-ization. Inside of this system, the vast amount of soil-enriching techniques are ignored and replaced with continuous applications of three water-soluble fertilizers: nitrogen, phos-phorus, and potassium (N-P-K). Biological life in the soil is greatly reduced, compromising its health and integrity.

Once this problem has begun below the surface, symptoms begin to arise in the plant bodies. Suddenly the plant's natural resistance to pests, fungus, and disease has been com-promised, leaving it open and vulnerable to attack. This problem is treated in conventional agriculture with the application of a wide range of pesticides and fungicides. The results seem effective. Fewer bugs, less disease, less overall damage to the plant. To the naked eye, the soil still looks brown and the plant still looks green. It seems like an efficient, effective method of controlling these unwanted variables. Unfortunately, as the soil continues to be ignored, vegetables are given heavier and heavier applications of these toxic substances. Eventually the chemicals have to be so hazardous that special suits and masks need to be used to apply them. At this point, if you were to take a closer look under the surface, you would notice the loss of biological life and the eventual death of the soil. Once all of the microbial life has been killed, no amount of nitrogen, phosphorus, or potassium can bring it back. Soil that was once rich and fertile becomes unsuitable for agriculture. The soil has become something to treat rather than something to build and strengthen. This is mirrored in the way that modern medicine cares for the human body. Much time is spent addressing a patient's symptoms rather than looking at the cause. As viruses are getting stronger, so are pests. We keep increasing the dosage only to find that the root of the problem still exists and the symptoms are getting harder and harder to treat. Some have found a more holistic approach—looking at the whole body, the whole farm, the whole earth—to be the solution for both human health and agriculture. It is becoming more and more of a mainstream idea that healthy food and an active lifestyle help with the longevity and health of humans.

Health and Harvesting

How produce is treated during harvest will play a role in how quickly it starts losing nutritional value. No matter what the vegetable, as soon as a plant is harvested it starts to degrade. The more the cellular structure of the plant is damaged during this process, the faster the loss of its nutrients. To keep its nutritional integrity, one should put as little stress on the plant during harvest as possible. Vegetables should be individually harvested in the coolest part of the day and quickly brought into refrigeration. You can see why scale is so important here. The larger the farm, the less attention is paid to each vegetable and the ideal harvesting circumstances it requires. Quality of produce is often superseded by the vast quantities needed to be harvested. In contrast, the small farmer is able to skillfully harvest each vegetable, keeping as much of its nutrition intact as possible.

After vegetables have been harvested, they go through the packing and transportation stage. During this process, the temperature at which the produce is being held determines the speed in which it loses its nutrients. Evidence of this is shown by Penn State researchers Luke LaBorde and Srilatha Pandrangi. Their testing was on the speed of nutrient loss in spinach after harvest. It showed that the warmer spinach is held, the quicker it loses its nutritional value. Their research showed that even when held at a steady 39 degrees F (refrigeration temperatures), most of its nutrients were lost after eight days.

Based on this research, much of the produce available to us has already lost the majority of its nutritional value. This is especially true when we are looking at perishable greens. Even on the West Coast, where much of the country's produce is grown, the majority of the vegetables sold in stores are already several days old. When you look at the extra time it takes to ship all over the country, you can start seeing why local food is so important. The average time that it takes our produce to get from the fields into our homes has increased exponentially in the last century as our farms have become fewer and farther away. Not only does this affect the nutritional content of the produce available to us but it also has a substantial environmental impact with the fossil fuel consumption it requires.

Nutritional Independence and Microgreens

Growing your own microgreens gives you the chance to bring a piece of the small farm into your own home. In essence, it gives you a slice of nutritional independence. You can have year-round access to fresh greens, even in the middle of winter. All of the factors that can limit nutrition are within your control. You are able to choose a soil that is filled with a diversity of ingredients. Using high-quality soil will ensure an abundance of minerals and trace elements are available to your greens. Harvesting is on your schedule. You can use sharp scissors during the coolest hours of the day to keep the nutrition intact. You can harvest to suit your needs and allow the rest of the tray to continue to grow. The packing and transportation stage is virtually nonexistent, leaving you with the freshest, most nutrient-dense greens available. You can take "local" to a whole new level, providing yourself and your family with microgreens all year long at the fraction of the price of greens from the store.

It can be difficult, over the course of an average week, to consume a wide variety of quality vegetables. During the winter months, finding fresh local produce can be particularly challenging. This has led to the growing popularity of supplements. People are very busy and often replace whole-food nutrition with convenient substitutes. Although many brands of supplements have incorporated techniques to try to retain peak nutritional value, nothing beats real food. Microgreens combine convenience and quality. They provide the quick and easy nourishment we need in our busy lives. The health benefits of these greens do not begin and end with their consumption. Taking a few moments out of the week to put your hands in the soil, spread some seed, and watch your greens grow can deepen and enrich your connection with your food and the earth. Although often overlooked, the health of our spirit must also be nourished. Being a part of something as fundamental as the life cycle of a plant gives us this opportunity. We can reconnect with our heritage and be stewards of the soil in our one tray of microgreens. We can slow down to the speed of plants and enjoy the subtle nuances of water, air, and sunlight until we return again to the rhythm of our lives.

Cruciferous Vegetables and Cancer Prevention

There have been countless studies done showing the link between cancer prevention and the consumption of cruciferous vegetables (i.e., all brassicas: broccoli, cabbage, arugula, etc.). The crystalline compounds (indoles) found in cruciferous vegetables have a range of health benefits. Studies have shown a significant reduction of cases of lung, breast, colon, ovarian, and bladder cancer in people who eat a diet high in these vegetables. They contain an estrogen stabilizer, diindolylmethane (DIM), which is important for both men and women. The balance that this compound creates results in greater resistance to cancer as well as the encouragement of overall hormone balance. Cancer growth can be spurred by certain estrogen metabolites active in the body. DIM acts as a deactivator, stopping growth. There has also been extensive research done on the effects of the phytonutrient sulfuraphane, which is also abundant in cruciferous vegetables. This powerful phytonutrient aids in detoxification, jump-starting the liver's natural tendency to flush the system. Unfortunately, it is hard to consume the quantities of cruciferous vegetables needed to reap the benefits. Enter microgreens. Studies have shown that one-and-a-half cups of full-grown broccoli has the same amount of this phytonutrient as just one ounce of broccoli four days after it has germinated. It is believed that the young broccoli has twenty to fifty times as much sulfuraphane as the fully grown. Makes you want to eat your brassicas, doesn't it?

MATERIALS

Growing microgreens requires only a few supplies. Some of these things you might already have around the house, while others will be just a minimal investment.

Trays

Due to the short period of time microgreens spend in their container, any shallow receptacle can be used to grow them. We find that standard 20 x 10-inch black plastic trays work well. These trays are often available at stores selling gardening supplies for around two dollars per tray. If you have a local nursery, you could check to see if they have any trays that would otherwise be thrown away. Especially in the spring, we have found that our local nursery gets small packs of annual flowers held in the same size trays and have no use for them. We have hundreds of trays that would have been an added investment if we hadn't found this niche. They are stackable, lightweight, reusable, and fairly durable. Even when they start cracking they can be reused by stacking two together.

Wood is another alternative. If you feel inspired to make your containers out of wood, they would work just as well. You could even use an old baking pan; you would just need to cut a few holes in the bottom for drainage. What you are looking for is a shallow, lightweight, movable tray.

Another option is using a shallow flower pot. There are a few factors to be aware of when choosing a pot to grow your microgreens. Although easy to find, clay pots can hinder germination because of their tendency to dry out quickly and wick moisture from the soil. Choose a wide shallow pot over a large tall pot to maximize the surface area for your growing greens and minimize unnecessary extra soil use. You may want to use several pots as your yield will probably be less than if you were using a standard tray.

Whether you decide to use wood, plastic, or metal, proper drainage is very important. Although often overlooked, drainage is one of the keys for a plant to thrive. While being very important in the garden, it is even more important in your trays. If you are buying or collecting plastic trays, they will probably already have holes cut in the bottoms. If you are making your own trays, be sure to create slits or holes to allow excess water to flow through. If there is a lack of drainage, you will find stunted growth, rot, and mold in your greens.

Soil

The heart of any farm or garden is its soil, and microgreens are no exception. Choosing the proper soil to grow your microgreens in is vital. A rich, fertile soil is teeming with the biological and mineral interactions necessary for vibrant, nutrient-rich plants. Apart from a few elements acquired from the atmosphere, plants draw all of their nutrition from the soil and water.

During our first season of growing microgreens, we used several brands of potting soil, looking for the best. Throughout these trials we were astounded to see the differences between them. All of the soils that we used were labeled "organic" with ingredients such as earthworm castings, bat guano, compost, etc. As our greens grew in these mediums, we quickly noticed dramatic differences in germination, growth, and overall health of the plants. Most of the cheaper soils touting the same ingredients fell short when it came to sustaining the dense growth of the greens.

The soil that stood out in both quality and performance had additional ingredients derived from the ocean such as kelp, crab meal, and shrimp meal. While you could use a lesser-quality soil for other things, your microgreens will often demand more. Using a high-quality soil, you will enjoy strong, even growth and an increased yield. While yield per tray is less important for the home grower, a commercial grower must pay close attention to this detail. The cost of higher-quality soil is often absorbed by the yields you will reap from your trays. We suggest going to your local nursery or horticultural store and spending some time looking at the available options. Talk with the shop keepers and choose a few brands of potting soil to take home and experiment with. Make sure the bags are labeled with their ingredients so you know what you are getting.

Soil Press

After filling your trays with soil, you will need a tool to create a flat seed bed. When we first experimented with growing these greens, we cut a thick piece of cardboard in the shape of our trays. It worked well for the short term but in the long run became soggy and damaged from weather and wet trays. If sowing just a few trays at a time, cardboard is a good option, but you may need to replace it every once in a while. Cardboard is easy to find and is usually free.

As our operation grew, we needed a more permanent press. Instead of making another out of the same material, we found some wood scraps and constructed a press with a handle.

Seeds

Quality seeds are another integral part of growing microgreens. Factors that will affect the viability of your seeds are storage, handling, age, and seed source. If you sow one thousand seeds, the difference between a 95-percent germination rate and a 50-percent germination rate is quite noticeable. It can be disheartening to have gone through the effort of sowing and caring for your trays only to see a small percentage of your seeds come up.

When it comes to storing and handling your seeds, you will want to keep them cool and dry. Avoid great fluctuation in temperature and moisture. During hot, humid summer days, be mindful not to leave them in the sun or let them get caught in a summer thunderstorm. Properly caring for your seeds will maintain their viability for a longer period of time.

Your seed packets offer you valuable information such as germination rate, age, and seed variety. Unless kept in a special environment, your seeds will last two to five years depending on the vegetable. The amount of time that your seeds will stay viable is an average and depends on whether you keep them in proper conditions.

With access to the Internet, you have hundreds of seed companies at your fingertips. For the purpose of growing microgreens, you are looking for seed companies selling in bulk. Many companies will sell only small packets of seeds, which is what you would find at your local gardening store. When trying out a new company, start with a small quantity of seed. If requested, many companies will provide free samples. When you have found the varieties you like, you will probably want to move up to quarter-pound bags. If you notice yourself going through seed quickly, most companies offer price breaks at one and five pounds. Due to the volume of seed you will be going through, price is a consideration. Obviously the commercial grower will go through quite a bit more seed than the home grower. Therefore, they might want to shop around to find the best combination of quality and price.

As you are browsing through seed catalogs, you will notice some companies offering both organic and nonorganic varieties. While we always advocate supporting small, local, and organic sources of seeds, they are not always available or affordable. Above anything is the importance of finding untreated seeds from reputable, service-oriented seed companies.

Something unique about growing microgreens is the need for seeds that not only have a high germination rate but also germinate at the same time. We have noticed with some of

Seeds	Average Years Viable
Amaranth	2
Arugula	3
Broccoli	4
Beet	4
Cabbage	4
Celery	3
Chard	4
Cress	5
Endive	5
Mustard	4
Pac Choi	3
Pea	3
Radish	5
Tokyo Bekana	3

Seed Viability Chart

our seed stock what we call "wave germination." With these seeds there is a difference in the timing of germination within the same sowing. We have noticed as much as two to three days between the first and last seeds germinating. This phenomenon would usually go unnoticed by most people growing full-sized vegetables. However, since we are harvesting our greens just one to two weeks after germination, we need all of our seeds to "pop" at the same time.

Seed quality also plays a role after your seeds have come up. We have grown broccoli that had great germination but had terrible-looking cotyledons. We have had China Rose radish, which is normally a beautiful pink-stemmed microgreen, come up with white stems. We have also had purple cabbage range from dark purple to green. Some of these variations won't bother the home grower, but for the commercial grower these deviations can be frustrating.

Towels

Using cloth or paper towels is a quick and effective alternative to covering your seeds with soil. Usually one would cover a sown tray with a dusting of soil, enough to cover the seeds.

For the home grower, with access to a washing machine, cloth towels work well. We recommend a thin, lightweight cotton cloth. You will want to wash them frequently, as wet towels can build up mold and bacteria. In our commercial operation, paper towels have been extremely effective. With the amount of trays that we sow every week, using paper towels became a better alternative. Between composting and using them in our vermiculture bins, paper towels fit easily into our system. Just remember to purchase unbleached natural paper towels, as you don't want to be watering bleach and other chemicals onto your germinating seeds and soil. Whichever type of towel you use, its purpose will be to provide a covering layer to keep your seeds warm and moist until they germinate.

Watering: Hoses, Sprayers, and Watering Cans

If you have a small garden or houseplants, you may already have some of the supplies you'll need to water your greens. If you are growing outside, a garden hose and a sprayer with several settings will be important. Make sure you can adjust the strength of its spray. Out of all the settings provided on our sprayer, a medium shower has been the most effective. If you are going to be growing indoors, you'll need a watering can. Make sure it has an attachment that allows the water to sprinkle out rather than pour out in one stream.

Since you are growing the greens so densely, air circulation is very important. You don't want to water them so hard that they fall and mat. If this happens, the lack of air and excess water will cause them to rot. If you find that your greens have fallen, you can try gently brushing them upright with your hand, or in other words, "fluff" them. The key to good watering is to be gentle yet thorough.

The pH Meter

The measurement of acidity or alkalinity of a solution is pH. A pH meter is an important investment when growing microgreens. The pH of your water will determine how well your greens are able to access the nutrients in the soil. If the pH is too low or high, these nutrients get locked up and become unavailable to the plants. Meters range in price from eight to eighty dollars. Cheaper options rely on liquid solutions and color matching while the more expensive meters are often digital and can be placed directly in the water being tested. We cannot say enough about the importance of testing the pH of your water. We spent our first two seasons unaware of the specific water pH needs of many of our crops. We struggled with some crops such as beet, basil, and amaranth, uncertain of what was causing the inconsistencies we were encountering. We came across rot and poor growth in many of our trays and spent a lot of time changing different variables in our system so that we could correct these problems. Nothing seemed to help permanently. We would often see promising results, only to find that the same problems came back in future sowings. While buying soil at our local horticultural store, we spoke with the owner about our plight. He suggested testing and monitoring the pH of our water. We found out that our water was very alkaline, registering at an 8 on the meter. While some of our Asian greens have been able to tolerate this high pH, we discovered that the crops that we had been having trouble with preferred a much lower reading. Once we adjusted according to their needs, all rot, damping off, and poor growth ceased. It was like magic. Still, we are astounded at the difference balancing our pH has made for our greens.

Adjusting the pH requires playing a little with chemistry. There are several different organic products available for lowering or raising pH. A simple solution for lowering pH (increasing your water's acidity) is using a bit of lemon juice. Baking soda, powdered oyster shells, or powdered dolomite lime will raise your pH (increasing your water's alkalinity).

As we said earlier, once the pH is brought into the proper range for the crop, the plant is able to draw key nutrients from the soil. Now that we have begun taking care of this factor, we are able to grow our greens well into their true leaf stage. Instead of becoming stressed and stunted, the greens have come to a new level of beauty. Although it may seem like another step, we believe that monitoring your pH is well worth it and can give you impressive results. Crops sensitive to high pH are noted in the Individual Crops chapter.

Lids for Germination

If you do not have a greenhouse to grow in, you will need to invest in or invent lids to cover your trays. This creates a "mini greenhouse effect" and keeps temperature and moisture at a more consistent state than if your germinating seeds were exposed to open air. This is especially important in dry climates or in seasons when there is larger fluctuation between the night and day temperatures. If lids are not used, you may find your seed germination is greatly reduced, uneven, and much slower than covered trays. The extra expense is well worth it in order to get a good yield.

If purchasing your lids, any local horticultural supply store or nursery should carry them. If they are not available in your area, you can find them online. Refer to the resource section of this book for specific Web sites. The average price seems to be around three dollars. Remember that you will want a lid that fits your container. One good thing about using a standard-size tray is that it is easy to find lids that will fit them. Keep this in mind if you decide to build your own trays or are using a flower pot. If you use a tray that is a different shape or size, you will need to create an alternative lid. For this you could use plastic bags or a pane of glass. If plastic lids are used, make sure they are stored in the shade to prevent melting and disfiguration of the plastic. If a pane of glass is used, keep the trays out of direct sun to avoid excess heat.

Heat Mats

Heat mats can provide extra warmth for warm-weather crops (such as amaranth or basil) or jump-start the germinating process of any seed. They are often unnecessary but can be especially helpful for starting seeds in colder climates. Relatively inexpensive, heat mats can be found at local horticultural stores or online, ranging in size and price. Heat mats are powered by electricity and gently warm the soil from below.

Scissors for Harvesting

We find that scissors are the most effective tool for harvesting microgreens. Buying a separate pair solely for the use of harvesting is not a bad idea—that way they stay sharp and clean and make cutting easy. Having a couple of different sizes of scissors can be helpful for cutting different varieties and densities of greens as well. The most important thing here is sharpness. Once your scissors begin to dull, you can either buy a new pair or sharpen your existing pair.

After years of trying different sharpeners for our knives and scissors, we have recently found one that is highly effective. The difficulty with most manual sharpeners is keeping the bevel at a consistent angle while you sharpen. If you do not keep the angle of the bevel consistent, it becomes more and more difficult over time to maintain a razor-sharp blade. The sharpener we have recently found clamps to the back of any size knife or scissor blade and will allow you to sharpen it at a constant angle. This takes any guesswork out of keeping your blade sharp. For more information on how to find a sharpener, take a look at the Recommended Books and Resources in the back of this book.

Making a clean cut through the stem is one important component to the longevity of your greens. The less cell damage done during the harvest, the longer they will hold. Once scissors are allowed to dull, they will start to tear the stems of the greens versus making a clean cut. If stored for later use, you may notice deterioration and discoloration at the bottom of the stem where they have been poorly cut.

Scale

A scale is essential only for those planning to sell their greens. You will find many options available online or at local restaurant supply stores. They will range in price from forty to four hundred dollars. When choosing your scale, precision is the most important factor. As you will be dealing in ounces and fractions of ounces, you will want to find a scale that will give you a reading of $1/10$-ounce increments.

Fan

Any small standard house fan with a few settings to choose from will work well for drying greens you plan to store or sell. You will want to choose one that either rests on the ground or has a pivoting head so that it can be pointed directly on your drying greens. We recommend a low to medium setting that won't overdry your delicate microgreens.

Storage Containers

You have a few options for storing your harvested greens. If you are planning to sell your greens to others, you can use either food-grade resealable bags or plastic clamshells. Both of these are available in bulk from various suppliers. For greens grown for home use, any bag or sealable container will work. Treat your microgreens as you would any delicate salad green.

HOW-TO-GROW
TEN-STEP PROCESS

Growing microgreens is a simple process that can be done in ten steps. You will discover that it takes little time, energy, and experience. You will quickly become skilled and efficient as you integrate the growing of fresh, nutritious greens into your life.

Step 1: Filling Your Trays With Soil

Now you are ready to grow microgreens! The first step is to fill your trays with the growing medium that you have chosen, creating the seed bed. We find that filling the trays with about an inch to an inch and a half of soil is sufficient. Use your hand to level out the soil. Make sure not to fill your trays to the very top to avoid soil and seed spilling over the edges when you first water. Use your soil press to smooth and flatten the soil, being mindful not to compact your seed bed. Over compaction will result in poor, slow growth.

Step 2: Sowing Your Seeds

Now that you have a smooth, even seed bed, you are ready to sow your seeds. Take a small pinch of seeds with your fingertips and sprinkle them over your tray using the same motion as if you were spicing a dish in the kitchen. Take your time to evenly spread the seeds over the entire tray. If you find that you have sown too many or too few seeds in any portion of the tray, simply add more seed or spread out the excess. You can either stick to one variety for your entire tray or sow as many types of seed as you like,

creating a mixed tray. This is nice if you are sowing only a couple trays at a time but still would
like a variety of greens to eat. The only thing to
be aware of when growing a mixed tray is to
use varieties that are able to be harvested at
approximately the same time.

The density of sowing depends on the seed
variety and the size at which you would like to harvest. If you want a dense tray of cotyledons, we
recommend broadcasting a thick layer of seed.

If you would like to experiment with growing your greens to their "true leaf" stage, simply
sow them less densely and allow them to grow for a longer period of time. In the beginning,
it may take some experimenting to get your sowing down. You may find that you have sown
some varieties too densely and are encountering poor growth and rot in your trays. On the
other extreme, if you have sown them too sparsely, your yield per tray will be very low. Soil
quality also plays a role in sustaining the growth of your greens. Start out with just a few
trays and find your balance. Once your tray has been sown, you will want to give it a light
pressing. The objective is to very lightly seat your seed in the soil, again being mindful not to
compact it. Seating your seed ensures that your seeds have contact with the soil so that they
can easily set roots.

Step 3: Covering Your Seeds

For this step you have three options. Traditionally,
one would cover his or her seeds with soil; a layer
about the depth of whichever seed is being sown,
but making sure the seed is covered. Another
option is to cover with cloth or paper towels. Your
third option is to leave your seeds uncovered if
you are germinating them in a dark place. Out
of these three methods, we believe covering trays
with towels to be the easiest and most effective.

Covering with Soil

If you to choose to cover with soil, smaller seeds (i.e., brassicas, endive, amaranth, etc.) will require you to cover them with sifted soil. While soil sifters are available, we find that using a pasta strainer works just as well and can be found in most kitchens. Simply put a handful of soil in the strainer and shake it over your trays. After doing this you will be left with the larger pieces of your potting soil that won't fit through your strainer. Set these aside and repeat this step until your seeds are covered. When covering your larger seeds (i.e., pea, chard, beet, etc.), sifting is unnecessary. Just take a handful of soil and sprinkle an even layer over the tray. After you have covered your tray, you will want to give it another gentle pressing. Apply the same amount of pressure as when seating your seed. If you find that once you have watered your trays you are starting to see seeds on the surface, just sprinkle a little more soil over the top.

Covering with Towels

An alternative to covering with soil is to use cloth or paper towels. While we don't use this method for most large seeds, it is extremely effective for covering smaller seeds. Laying a towel over your sown trays creates a moisture blanket. Take your lightweight cotton or paper towel and lay it directly on your seeds. Once in place, keep moist until the seeds have germinated.

After our first season, we started experimenting with towels. We found that the towels had all the benefits of covering with soil and none of the drawbacks. This method started saving us time and money. We cut our soil costs and saved time covering our trays. Towels also allow you to sneak a peek into the day-to-day progress of your germinating seeds. This can be entertaining to children, as they can look under the towel and watch the seeds slowly open and develop into plants.

Uncovered Seeds

With this method you are not covering the seeds with anything. This means more time must be spent monitoring moisture to ensure germination. Your trays will need to be under some kind of protection, whether it be a greenhouse or lids. It will also be helpful to keep these trays out of direct sunlight, especially in the summer. This will help with maintaining adequate moisture. If you choose to leave the seeds uncovered, pay careful attention when seating them.

Step 4: Initial Watering

The next step is to water your trays. Set your sprayer to a light/medium shower setting so that the entire tray gets gently soaked. Preliminary watering is the only stage at which overwatering is not an issue as long as your seeds are not drowning in water. However, underwatering will result in poor or no germination. A germinating seed must remain moist. If the seed bed, and therefore the seed, is allowed to dry out, the process will halt and your seeds will no longer be viable.

Step 5: Cover with Lids

Once your trays have been watered, you will need to cover them with lids if you are not growing in a greenhouse of some sort. The reason for using these lids is to speed up germination by holding in heat and retaining moisture. Keep in mind that if using plastic lids, you will want to keep a close eye on your trays when in direct sunlight. Due to the "mini greenhouse effect" that the lids create, temperatures inside can become substantially greater than the air outside. This is a benefit for stimulating germination and growth, but it must be monitored in order

to avoid excess buildup of heat in your trays. If you notice that things are a bit too steamy inside, simply move the lid slightly to the side to create some ventilation.

Step 6: Watering Your Germinating Seeds

As your seeds are germinating, it is important to keep a close eye on their progress and to maintain proper moisture. When using the towel method, observe the dampness of the towel and water daily, keeping the towel and the seed below it moist. One benefit of the towel method is that it gives you a window into the germination process. Instead of the seeds being hidden from your view, you can lift a corner of the towel at any time, allowing you to watch the stages of germination. You want your seeds to remain covered until they are fully germinated. After a few days, you will notice that the towels will have started to lift off the soil, giving you a hint that your greens are getting ready to need to see the light. As illustrated in the photographs, certain germinating seeds acquire a white fuzz on their stems. This is not mold and is a natural part of the process as your seedlings set roots.

Trays covered with soil will require a bit more attention. Soil will

Stage 1

Stage 2

dry out more quickly than towels, so make sure these trays are watered a couple of times a day. With microgreens, your trays will be so densely sown that when they germinate, the covering layer of soil will lift with the seeds. If the soil is not evenly rinsed from the seeds early in this process, they will remain under the soil in darkness. These seedlings will quickly become weedy and pale. When watered at this point, the covering soil can drown and kill much of the tray. That said, we covered our seeds with soil our entire first season of growing our greens. While it is not difficult to do, losing trays because you are a few hours off can be frustrating.

Pulling Off Towel

If you choose not to cover your seeds, take caution when watering. A gentle shower will ensure that your germinating seeds aren't disrupted. Remember that whichever covering method you choose, your seeds will need consistent moisture to germinate.

Stage 3

Step 7: Finding A Good Spot To Grow

One thing that makes growing microgreens so accessible to so many people is the lack of space they require. People often refer to us as "porch farmers," as we are able to support our entire microgreen client base on less than 100 square feet. If you don't have enough room to plant a garden in the backyard or don't even have a backyard, a windowsill, porch, patio, or front step will provide plenty of space to grow fresh, delicious microgreens for yourself and your family.

As we all know, plants need light to thrive. The germination process, however, does not require light. This allows you to keep your germinating trays anywhere, so long as they are kept warm and moist. Once germinated, microgreens, like most other plants, require light to grow and flourish. This process of taking sunlight and converting it to energy is known as photosynthesis and is a fundamental process in the growth of your greens. Once your seeds have germinated, you will want to find a sunny spot inside or outside for them to grow.

Choosing the location of your trays requires paying attention to your greens. In the heat of the summer, some varieties may prefer full sun, while others require dappled shade. No matter what the variety, some amount of light and warmth are required. You will find that plants deprived of light will begin reaching for whatever light source they can find. They will then become "leggy" and scrawny as opposed to being strong, stout healthy-looking plants. You will also notice a change in their color. While the trays given enough light are looking like a dense lawn of richly colored greens, the trays deprived of light will begin looking yellow and weak, making them more susceptible to rot and disease. This is easily avoided. Let them see the light! Strive to find a place for your greens that provides the most amount of sunlight. A sunny windowsill, your porch ledge, or even your front step could all serve as great places to grow your greens.

If you feel you are unable to get adequate sunlight, grow lights are also an option. There are a variety of grow lights available from your local gardening store or online, ranging in size and price. Keep in mind your energy costs when purchasing a system. Living in sunny places, you may never use them, but they could be quite helpful in places where sunlight is scarce during the winter months. Grow lights can be set up anywhere that is convenient. A basement or unused closet could easily be transformed into a greens-growing haven.

Step 8: Maintaining Your Growing Greens

Now that your seeds have germinated, they will require light to grow and thrive. If you are using the towel method, you will now want to remove the towel and the plastic lid. Once the towel is removed, it can be composted, used in a vermiculture system, burned, or thrown away. If growing indoors, you can flip your lid over and place your tray inside. This will keep excess water off of your counters. Be sure to empty this water daily so that your soil isn't standing in water.

Depending on the variety, the greens will need to remain in the light for an average of seven to fourteen days. A fast-growing green like arugula will require a minimum growing period, while slow-growing basil will need more time. Keep in mind that weather, location, and watering patterns all play a role in this time-line. While you may go through several growing cycles with the same results, great variation does tend to occur if any of the previously named factors are altered. Should you decide to branch out after experimenting with some basic varieties, you will notice that more exotic microgreens such as mint or sorrel will take substantially longer to both germinate and grow to size. Specific data on average germination and growth times for a number of crops is located in the Individual Crops chapter of this book.

Since your seedlings are now out in the light, you must pay attention to their moisture. Merely looking at the surface of the soil will not give you an accurate reading of its moisture content. You will need to get your hands dirty. Stick your finger in the corner of the tray to make sure that all of the soil is wet. Watering once a day is often sufficient—just be careful not to overwater. Overwatering at this stage can drown the seedlings and stop the growth process. Underwatering will result in wilted greens. Once their cellulose structure has been compromised by either over- or underwatering, the greens may remain

damaged but are often able to recover. You might notice this if you have chosen a poorly lit place for your greens and later relocated them. You could also leave your greens during a cloudy day, thinking you have watered them sufficiently, only to find that it is sunny when you return and your greens have wilted. Often, a gentle soaking will revive them after a couple of hours.

This phenomenon occurs all the time in nature, especially in hot, dry climates where plants must preserve their energy. If facing intense direct sun and thereby heat, energy is sent to the roots to sustain the life of the plant, allowing the leaves and flowers to droop and wilt during the heat of the day. One could come upon such a plant midday and think it was dying, only to find the same plant in its full glory during the coolest part of the evening. That said, you want to avoid as much stress on your greens as possible, keeping them properly watered. Take note of the strength of the sun and avoid watering midday. When plants are watered in the heat of the day, the drops of water act as little magnifying glasses and can burn the leaves. This is easily avoided by watering either in the morning or evening in climates and times of year when the sun is at its strongest.

Step 9: Harvesting

When to Harvest

Microgreens can be harvested at different stages of growth. You can either harvest them just after their cotyledons have opened or wait for them to put on a second set of leaves, known as true leaves. If allowed to continue to grow, eventually the greens will begin to show signs of stress such as yellowing, stunted growth, and looking weak or "leggy" (tall and unhealthy), and they will start to rot from underneath. This generally starts to happen because of how densely you are sowing the seeds and the small amount of soil you are growing them in. If the same seed were allowed to grow less densely, in a bigger container or directly in the ground with plenty of room for its roots, you could watch it grow through many stages. Depending on the variety, it would eventually grow into a full-sized plant from which you might harvest its fruit or leaf (i.e., a head of broccoli or full-grown leaves of arugula). Soil quality also plays a major role in the health and vitality of your greens. If you are using a lesser-quality soil, signs of stress will become apparent much earlier and more frequently.

How to Harvest

When getting ready to harvest your greens, one of the most important factors to be aware of is the heat of the day. Cutting the greens while they have been in the sun for a few hours or even in the shade during a hot summer's day will result in wilted greens that will quickly turn to mush. You can always try soaking them in cold water to revive them, but they are usually too far gone to perk back up. Early mornings and evenings are the ideal times to harvest. The key here is to keep your greens cool. Harvesting at the proper time will keep them looking as fresh and alive as when they were growing. This is especially important for greens you plan to sell to others or store for yourself.

We find that scissors make the most effective tool for harvesting microgreens. Think of cutting your tray like giving your greens a haircut. Hold a section loosely with one hand and use the other hand to snip with your scissors. Your greens may range from one to four inches tall, depending on the variety and age at which they are cut. To get a nice ratio of greens and stem, cut about one inch above the soil for most greens. If the greens have been allowed to get tall or you prefer less stem, cut higher up. After your cut, take the greens in one hand

and loosely flick the stem side of the cut to knock off any soil or damaged ends. This step will keep your home salad clean and will save time washing if you are planning on selling your greens. After cutting, put each handful in a bowl or on a plate and use as much as you need. Unless you are cutting above the cotyledons, your trays will not grow again. The remaining soil and roots can be composted. The chapter on composting will give you more information on "recycling" your used soil.

We harvest our greens differently if we are cutting to sell or if we are making a home salad. When harvesting for our restaurant orders, we use a small digital scale and zero out the weight of a plate to get accurate weights as we are cutting. We usually harvest a bit more than we need to account for lost weight after washing.

When we are harvesting for ourselves it's much more casual. Obviously we do not use a scale and often snip a bit from several trays, making a custom salad as we like it. Don't feel like you have to harvest a whole tray or harvest from only one variety at a time. You can also experiment with greens at different stages of growth and create a unique mix by using just a couple of varieties at different sizes. This will provide different textures and a varied look to your mix.

One of the greatest things we find about growing microgreens is the ability to cut and eat them within minutes. This allows you to have the freshest, tastiest, and most nutritious salad available right from your own home. In Recipes: Food as Art (page 129), we describe different mixes we like and pair them with recipes for you to explore, but keep in mind that your only limitations are your taste buds and imagination.

Step 10: Washing and Storage

Washing

Unless you are planning on selling your greens to restaurants or individuals, it is often unnecessary to wash them. You can treat them as you would salad greens from your garden or the store by giving them a quick rinse before serving them.

Some growers choose not to wash their greens before they sell them. In operations where soil-less methods are used (i.e., hydroponics), selling unwashed greens is more of an option. However, if growing with soil, washing the greens is important so that you can offer a clean product, free of soil and rotten leaves. The process of washing the greens gives you a closer look at your product and allows you to remove any soil, debris, seed hulls, or rotten leaves before you sell it to your client. This will give you the confidence of knowing exactly what you are selling as well as an edge over any competition selling unwashed greens.

The process of washing microgreens is simple but can also be tedious and time consuming. We find that purchasing a plastic tub to use solely for washing greens is convenient.

You will want to find a size that fits in the sink where you will be washing to have easy access to running water. Wash your greens in cold water to maintain freshness. Proper lighting is important so that you can get a good look at your harvest and remove any duff or rotten leaves easily. We find that a well-lit room and the use of a headlamp makes this process

much easier. Technique varies in the cleaning of greens. Most of the seed hulls, seeds, duff, and damaged leaves float to the top, where they can be easily skimmed off using your hand. Soil and other heavy particles often sink to the bottom. This process takes an eye for detail and a great deal of patience. In order to really showcase your greens, we find it important to be impeccable with your processing. While this may seem daunting at first, with practice, you will become both skilled and efficient. You may find that you invent new methods that help you to streamline processing. Different crops often call for different methods. While some greens are effortless to wash, others prove more difficult and require more time and attention. We have found that greens that are especially dirty or full of damaged leaves require a two-stage washing method. After the initial washing, we take out a handful at a time, examine it on a plate, pull out anything we have missed and continue until finished. Often, these greens will require a second rinse. If you choose to use the "towel method" for covering your germinating seeds, they will require far less washing than if covered with soil. Covering with towels eliminates half of the soil and seed hull normally found in your rinse water, thereby cutting your work in half. When we switched from covering with soil to covering with towels, we went from three to four rinses per crop down to one or two.

Drying

After your greens have been washed, your next step is drying. Using a small fan is very effective. You will want to use your fan on a low to medium setting and be sure to keep an eye on the greens. You will need to turn and fluff them every few minutes, being careful not to overdry them. Your beautiful, delicate microgreens can turn quite the opposite if allowed to become over- or underdried and stored in the refrigerator.

Storing

If you are storing your greens for yourself, we recommend using a resealable bag, filled with a bit of air, and putting it directly in the refrigerator. Another option is using a reusable container. Although quite perishable, microgreens will last at least three to four days and often up to a week or more, depending on their quality, variety, and the amount of moisture in the container.

If your greens are being sold, you will want to invest in a small accurate scale and either food-grade resealable plastic bags or plastic clamshells (resources available in the back of the book). We find selling four-ounce packages to be convenient for both the chef and the grower. Creating a label of some kind is useful to distinguish the date the greens were harvested as well as their variety.

Scale of Production

Home Grower

When deciding how many trays to grow, your first consideration will be how many people you would like to feed. Every home has people who eat a varying amount of greens; therefore, the number of trays you need will also vary. For a family of four, we would start with two to three trays, twice a week. Because the growing cycle is so short, it is easy to start small and adjust accordingly. Each tray can be sown with a few different varieties to have an enjoyable assortment of colors, flavors, and textures. You will generally have a batch of trays that you are harvesting from, a batch that is germinating, and a batch you are sowing. This will allow for the constant flow of fresh greens for the home. If you're growing for just yourself, or space is a consideration, sowing even one tray a week would be great. Having a small influx of fresh homegrown greens for the family is priceless.

Commercial Grower

If you want to sell your greens to restaurants or individuals, start small. This will allow you time to work out any kinks, choose varieties that work for you, and get a sense of the average weight per tray. As with the home grower, sowing twice a week will allow for a constant flow of greens for your accounts. When we started our small operation, we took on one or two accounts at a time. This enabled us to get comfortable with supplying the new demand. As the season progresses, you will notice that your chefs will have their favorites and will also want new varieties to try. Once again, the short growing cycle and frequent sowings will easily accommodate any fluctuation in your orders.

INDIVIDUAL CROPS

This chapter will highlight a range of vegetables that can be grown as microgreens. There are many more varieties that can be experimented with, but these will provide you with a platform to branch out from. Keep in mind that the averages provided for days to germination and harvest are based on growing temperatures ranging from 65 to 75 degrees F. Use these averages as a guide and adjust according to your climate. The weight ranges that we obtain are based on using standard 20 x 10-inch black plastic trays. Remember this when you are comparing weights of a homemade or alternative vessel.

Don't be limited by the crops listed in this chapter. Many vegetables and herbs make great microgreens. One rule of thumb when choosing vegetable varieties is to avoid fruiting vegetables such as squash, tomatoes, etc., and lean towards leafy crops such as kale or collards. You will find that some vegetables are more suited than others. Experiment! Herbs make very interesting microgreens. You can try everything from chervil to chives. While herbs tend to take a long time to germinate and grow to size, they add exciting flare to the home grower's kitchen. Johnny's Selected Seeds in Maine (www.johnnyseeds.com) offers an extensive list of microgreen options that can be helpful in spurring your imagination.

While there are a few different methods used to grow microgreens (i.e. aeroponics, hydroponics), our experience is with using high-quality organic potting soil and our data reflects the use of that medium. If you are interested in using either of the other methods, your weights and appearances may vary. We are soil lovers and have not spent any time or energy learning about hydroponics or aeroponics, but there are plenty of people who have gotten good results and there is ample information on these techniques online.

Amaranth

Family	Amaranthaceae
Genus and species	*Amaranthus cruentus*
Varieties we recommend	Red Garnet
Taste	Slightly earthy
Average days to germinate	2 to 3 days
Average days to harvest (after germination)	8 to 12 days
Average weight per tray	2 to 3 ounces
Difficulty	Medium to difficult

Growing Tips

- Amaranth requires consistency. Fluctuation in temperature results in slow or low germination as well as poor growth after germination.
- Traditionally grown as a grain in dry climates, amaranth doesn't like constant soil saturation.
- You can harvest it at the cotyledon stage or allow it to mature and grow true leaves for a different texture.
- Amaranth is a summer crop and prefers the heat, avoid growing it in the winter months.
- The towel method works well with this small seed.
- Keep your water under a pH of 7.

Harvesting Tips

- Harvest close to the soil.
- Amaranth is very lightweight and is generally used solely as a splash of color rather than contributing to the weight of a mix.

Washing Tips

- When harvested young, amaranth can be tricky to wash. It is so light and small that the leaves may float through your fingers. We recommend using a small hand-held strainer to process this crop. If you allow it to mature, a strainer will be unnecessary.
- It can be tedious to separate the tiny beige seed hulls from the magenta greens. Use your hand to remove any seed hulls from the sides of your washing receptacle.

Possible Challenges

- Overwatering and inconsistent temperatures can lead to poor germination and growth, as well as rot.
- Take extra care with this crop.
- Amaranth hates an alkaline soil, and a pH over 7 will result in rotting.

Our Thoughts

Ranging from bright magenta at its cotyledon stage to a deeper purple when forming its true leaves, amaranth is the key to our most popular mix. It is stunning at any stage and creates rich, brilliant contrast. Amaranth maintains its vibrant color in both its stem and cotyledon, making it a unique asset to your repertoire.

Brief History

Native to the Americas, amaranth was a staple to some of the great civilizations of Central and South America. Amaranth was thought of as a "super grain" and was rotated in the fields with maize and beans. Since its early cultivation, amaranth has seen great decline in its production. Although the reason for the diminishment of this nutritious grain is largely up to speculation, theories include inconvenient small-seed size or modernization in agriculture. Aztec lore attributes its decline to an attempt by the Spanish conquistadors to eradicate amaranth because of its key role in traditional Aztec sacrifices. It is thought that it has prevailed thus far partly due to its beauty. The entire plant features an unmistakable vibrant magenta color not found in many crops today. While still unknown by much of the U.S. population, amaranth has begun growing in popularity since the 1980s for its high protein content and overall health benefits.

Arugula

Family	Brassicaceae
Genus and species	Eruca sativa
Varieties we recommend	Standard Arugula, Astro
Taste	Sharp, peppery, spicy
Average days to germinate	2 to 3 days
Average days to harvest (after germination)	5 to 7 days
Average weight per tray	4 to 6 ounces
Difficulty	Easy

Growing Tips

- Easy and fast to grow.
- Can germinate in temperatures as low as 40 degrees F.
- Towel method helps with seeds sticking to leaves.
- True leaves can be difficult to obtain if pH is over 7.

Harvesting Tips

- Generally quick and easy to harvest.
- Lack of air flow makes this crop susceptible to rot. If rotting occurs, be mindful to avoid these patches when harvesting.

Washing Tips

- Can be tedious to wash, especially if covered with soil.
- Arugula has a mucilaginous seed, which makes it cling to the bottom of its cotyledons.
- We recommend using the two-stage washing method.
- Using the towel method also helps pull away seed hulls.

Possible Challenges

- Arugula's thin stem makes it more apt to fall and mat when being watered. Water lightly and if they fall, gently brush them back up.
- Mucilaginous seed can make washing time consuming.

Our Thoughts

One of the more common microgreens, arugula's spicy flavor and pretty heart-shaped leaf make it great on its own or as the base of a mix. Arugula's strong familiar taste also makes it a great addition to larger salad mixes. Its quick germination and growth make it accessible for just about anyone to grow.

Brief History

Like many other spicy, pungent vegetables, arugula was thought to have aphrodisiac qualities. Records date early use back to the first century. In addition to its peppery leaves, arugula seeds were also a resource for adding their distinct flavor to oils. Commonly referred to as "rocket" or "roquette" in England, it has been revered for its strong flavor and medicinal qualities. With health claims ranging from curing freckles to acting as a natural deodorant, arugula certainly has more allure than just a simple salad green. In the United States, it has become increasingly familiar to our eyes and taste buds as it has gained popularity in modern cooking since the early 1990s.

Basil

Family	Lamiaceae
Genus and species	*Ocimum basilicum*
Varieties we recommend	Dark Opal, Genovese, Sweet Italian
Taste	Potent, aromatic basil flavor
Average days to germinate	4 to 5 days
Average days to harvest (after germination)	14 to 21 days
Average weight per tray	2 to 4 ounces
Difficulty	Medium to difficult

Growing Tips

- Requires steady warm temperatures.
- Using a heat mat helps with germination when nighttime temperatures drop.

Harvesting Tips

- Basil is a low grower. Be sure to cut close to the soil to keep the full plant intact.
- Take your time during harvest to avoid capturing excess soil with your scissors.

Washing Tips

- Avoid washing unless very dirty.
- Basil is a very sensitive herb. If washed and stored in cold temperatures, it will blacken. If you are using it immediately, a quick rinse won't affect the leaves.
- To remove any dirt collected in the harvesting process, lay your harvest on a cotton cloth. Transfer the greens from the cloth to another cloth. Extra dirt tends to stick to the cloth instead of your basil. You can repeat this process several times, but be sure to handle the delicate basil with care to avoid bruising the leaves.

Possible Challenges

- Basil is a very delicate microgreen and bruises easily, so it requires extra care.
- Being a summer crop, it likes warm weather and will not tolerate great fluctuation in temperature.
- When storing, be sure to keep plenty of air in the bags to keep the basil from bruising and blackening.

Our Thoughts

Micro basil is gorgeous. Green varieties offer signature basil flavor in miniature form. It is a beautiful accent to many dishes and can even be incorporated into desserts. Purple basil can be used on its own or mixed with green to wow your eyes and your taste buds. Once you have overcome some of the challenges of growing micro basil, you will find that it makes ordinary dishes extraordinary and never disappoints in flavor.

Brief History

Basil in some form, fresh or dried, can be found in most kitchens today. It is a fairly versatile herb that has found its way into recipes from Italian to Thai cooking. A relative of mint, it is thought to have originated in Africa and Asia over five thousand years ago, eventually making its way to the United States by the early seventeenth century. Basil's strong flavor has made it the center of many different fables and folklore. For some reason there seems to be a strange connection between basil and scorpions. Medicinally, it was thought that basil could treat a scorpion sting. It was also common thought that if you left a basil leaf under a pot, it might turn into a scorpion itself or that simply eating basil might cause scorpions to grow in your brain! In Italy, it is thought of as a symbol of love, while in Mexico, it is said that basil will ensure a lover's eye doesn't wander. Both the leaf and the seed have been used medicinally. It has been thought to be a cure for many ailments, from intestinal issues to warts. Even today, research has been done on basil's anti-inflammatory and antibacterial effects. It also contains special components called flavonoids that offer protection at a cellular level. Basil has proven to be an asset to both your kitchen cupboard and medicine cabinet.

Beet

Family	Chenopodiaceae
Genus and species	*Beta vulgaris*
Varieties we recommend	Ruby Queen, Detroit Red, Red Ace
Taste	Earthy
Average days to germinate	4 to 6 days
Average days to harvest (after germination)	8 to 12 days
Average weight per tray	5 to 7 ounces
Difficulty	Medium to difficult

Growing Tips

- Soaking beet seeds for 24 hours helps with germination rate and speed.
- Adding a teaspoon of liquid kelp to the water is beneficial.
- Best results often occur if the first pressing of the soil is skipped. After broadcasting the seeds, press them lightly into the loose soil, and then cover with a towel or soil.
- Make sure that this large seed is completely covered so it stays moist.
- To obtain great germination, keep your beet at a steady temperature.
- After germination, avoid keeping soil too moist.
- Keep your pH under 7.

Harvesting Tips

- If most of the seedlings still have seed hulls attached to their leaves, wait a few more days to harvest.
- The large knobby seeds that remain can be gently pulled off before harvesting.
- Feature the bright stem of the beet by cutting close to the soil.

Washing Tips

- Beet's large seeds are easy to see in the wash water. When harvested young, you will find many seed hulls stuck to the leaves. Removing them can be time consuming but can be greatly reduced by being diligent while harvesting.
- We recommend the two-stage washing method to be sure to remove all hulls.

Possible Challenges

- Beet requires extra attention; monitor your pH to avoid rot.
- Overwatering will result in rotting.

Our Thoughts

Red beet's vibrant stem is unmistakable. It is stunning as a single crop or beautiful as a bright accent in any mix. Bull's Blood is the most widely known variety grown for microgreens and also one of the most expensive. While Bull's Blood yields a richly colored stem and a nice green, we have found that Ruby Queen is a reasonably priced alternative that offers similar qualities.

Brief History

The beet originated in the Mediterranean region, where it was used medicinally beginning before the written word. Beets were often used in Roman times for fever and constipation. Called the "blood turnip" in the nineteenth century, beets were also wild crafted for their leaves. Anyone who has eaten the modern-day beet might notice its distinctly earthy taste; this is due to special microbial life in the soil that creates an organic compound called geosmin.

Broccoli

Family	Brassicaceae
Genus and species	*Brassica oleracea*
Varieties we recommend	Standard Broccoli, DiCicco, Waltham
Taste	Cabbagelike
Average days to germinate	3 to 4 days
Average days to harvest (after germination)	5 to 7 days
Average weight per tray	5 to 7 ounces
Difficulty	Easy

Growing Tips

- One of the easier microgreens to grow.
- Sow thickly for heavy yields.
- It can get woody if allowed to grow to true leaf stage.

Harvesting Tips

- Easy and quick to harvest.
- Cut high on the stem to keep a balanced ratio of leaf to stem.

Washing Tips

- Easy and quick to wash.
- Often requires only one rinse.
- Seed hulls will gravitate to the edges of the washing tub for easy removal.

Possible Challenges

- None that we have found.

Our Thoughts

Broccoli's rich dark greens are a nice addition to any mix or are beautiful on their own. Broccoli microgreens, along with other cruciferous vegetables, offer many cancer fighting properties. They contain DIM (diindolylmethane) which has been shown to provide hormonal balance, an important factor in human health. Adding these microgreens to your diet is an easy way to obtain digestible DIM.

Brief History

Broccoli originated from wild cabbage, which is native to parts of Europe. It is not certain whether or not Romans cultivated it, but it is clear that it was being enjoyed in Italy well before the rest of the world. Broccoli is derived from the Italian word for "arm" (*braccio*). For much of its early history, broccoli was often confused with its parent plant cauliflower. Because of this lack of clarity, its history is not very well documented. Called sprouted or asparagus broccoli, early cultivars resembled more of a broccoli rabe than the tight treelike stalks we recognize today. It did not make it to North America until the early nineteenth century when it was brought by Italian immigrants, and it took another century for it to become widely known and accepted.

Purple Cabbage

Family	Brassicaceae
Genus and species	*Brassica oleracea*
Varieties we recommend	Red Acre, Red Mammoth, O.P. Red
Taste	Distinctive mild cabbage flavor
Average days to germinate	3 to 5 days
Average days to harvest (after germination)	4 to 7 days
Average weight per tray	4 to 6 ounces
Difficulty	Easy

Growing Tips

- Some varieties have a more vivid purple color than others.
- Cold or heat stress can create deeper purple shades.
- Becomes less purple with age.
- When harvested young, cabbage has a sweeter flavor and a more tender texture.

Harvesting Tips

- Very easy to harvest.
- If there is any rot or soil in your harvest, the darker purple color can make it more difficult to spot.

Washing Tips

- Because of cabbage's dark purple color, seed hulls can be difficult to spot.
- Again, spotting blackened leaves from rot can be challenging due to the leaf's dark color. The two-stage washing method can be helpful to save time and your eyes.
- When washing a healthy rot-free tray of cabbage, it is quick and easy, often requiring only one or two rinses.

Possible Challenges

- Cabbage's dark color can hide leaf flaws. While this is not a consideration for the home grower, it can slow down washing for the seller.

Our Thoughts

Cabbage's rich purple cotyledons and light purple stem make it unique and beautiful. It has a mild cabbage flavor, making it perfect as a base for a mix. Paired with bright yellows and the magenta of amaranth, cabbage makes for a beautiful canvas for light colors to pop. Cabbage microgreens, along with other cruciferous vegetables, offer many cancer fighting properties. They contain DIM (diindolylmethane) which has been shown to provide hormonal balance, an important factor in human health. Adding these microgreens to your diet is an easy way to obtain digestible DIM.

Brief History

Cabbage's ancestry links it to its wild form that resembled a modern-day kale because of the lack of its signature tight head. Wild cabbage is prehistoric. Believed to have been cultivated for thousands of years, it has served as both food and medicine. Cabbage was used on ships as a preventative against scurvy because of its high levels of vitamin C. Hailed as a cure for a hangover in Roman times and used as an anti-fungal and anti-inflammatory, its medicinal scope is broad reaching. Along with its health claims, cabbage has been an inexpensive staple enjoyed by many early Europeans. Varieties range in size, color, and appearance. Purple or red types can be used for dying, creating a fairly colorfast solution for dark purple using natural sources.

Celery

Family	Apiaceae
Genus and species	*Apium graveolens*
Varieties we recommend	Utah, Standard Cutting Celery
Taste	Surprisingly strong celery flavor
Average days to germinate	5 to 7 days
Average days to harvest (after germination)	14 to 17 days
Average weight per tray	2 to 4 ounces
Difficulty	Easy to medium

Growing Tips

- Celery is a slow grower. It can be slow to germinate and slow to mature.
- Because of its tiny cotyledons, it is a crop you will definitely want to grow to its true leaf stage.
- A delicate crop, celery can be easily stunted. When optimal conditions are compromised, it can begin to yellow and stop growing.
- Keep celery in consistent temperatures.
- Because of its small seed size, the towel method works well.
- Keep your pH under 7.

Harvesting Tips

- Harvest close to the soil.
- Celery micros are compact and very lightweight.
- Cut below the cotyledons to make sure you are harvesting the entire seedling with its true leaf.

Washing Tips

- Put on your spectacles for this one—celery micros are quite dainty and often hold onto their seed hulls.
- It can be challenging to get all of the little red celery seed hulls out of your wash water. This crop takes patience and a keen eye.
- The two-stage washing method with a couple of extra rinses is recommended.

Possible Challenges

- Stunted growth and yellowing may occur if pH is over 7.

Our Thoughts

Celery is worth growing for flavor alone. Although it doesn't weigh much for the commercial grower, it is an interesting and zesty crop that is often a hit with chefs or home cooks. Celery takes patience in all stages, but in the end, it doesn't disappoint.

Brief History

Celery is an ancient vegetable thought to have originated in the Mediterranean area. Native varieties have been found from Asia Minor to the southern tip of South America, making it hard to be sure. It has been found in Egyptian tombs, worn by Greek athletes, and used medicinally by many cultures. Celery seed was used in Ayurvedic medicine for everything from colds to arthritis. Through cultivation, wild celery's unappealing bitter taste was tamed and slowly started being appreciated as a culinary asset. By the early eighteenth century, celery had found its way into the soups and broths of England, Italy, and France.

Chard

Family	Chenopodiaceae
Genus and species	*Beta vulgaris*
Varieties we recommend	Rainbow Mix, Ruby Red
Taste	Similar to beet greens but sweeter
Average days to germinate	4 to 6 days
Average days to harvest (after germination)	8 to 12 days
Average weight per tray	4 to 6 ounces
Difficulty	Medium

Growing Tips

- Soaking chard seeds for 24 hours helps with germination rate and speed.
- Adding a teaspoon of liquid kelp to the water is beneficial.
- Best results often occur if the first pressing of the soil is skipped. After broadcasting the seeds, press them lightly into the loose soil, and then cover with a towel or soil.
- Make sure that this large seed is completely covered so it stays moist.
- To obtain great germination, keep your chard at a steady temperature.
- After germination, avoid keeping soil too moist.
- Keep your pH under 7.

Harvesting Tips

- If most of the seedlings still have seed hulls attached to their leaves, wait a few more days to harvest.
- The large knobby seeds that remain can be gently pulled off before harvesting.
- Feature the bright stem of the beet by cutting close to the soil.

Washing Tips

- Chard's large seeds are easy to see in the wash water. When harvested young, you will find many seed hulls stuck to the leaves. Removing them can be time consuming, but this can be greatly reduced by being diligent while harvesting.
- We recommend the two-stage washing method to be sure to remove all hulls.

Possible Challenges

- Chard requires extra attention; monitor your pH to avoid rot.
- Overwatering will result in rotting.

Our Thoughts

Chard, with its unobtrusive flavor, adds a colorful flair to any dish. The variety of colors in the rainbow mix makes it popular with chefs. Rainbow mix is nice on its own or as an addition to any mix. Any of the individual colors in the rainbow mix are available from most seed sources. This makes it possible to customize your chard mix, isolating the colors that you prefer.

Brief History

Chard and beet share the same genus and species. This is because they originate from the same plant, wild sea beet. As has been done for centuries, farmers have accentuated different parts of a plant through selective propagation. Instead of accentuating its root, chard has been allowed to grow broad leaves that can be used for cooking or eaten raw. Records date early cultivation back to 350 BC. Greeks are thought to have cultivated the *Beta vulgaris* species for its leaf by 400 BC. Traded all over the Mediterranean, it was enjoyed in a mass of colors and varieties. Specifics on its medicinal use are not very well documented, but it is thought to have been used chiefly for its medicinal properties in ancient times.

Cilantro (Coriander)

Family	Apiaceae
Genus and species	*Coriandrum sativum*
Varieties we recommend	Standard Cilantro, Santo
Taste	Very potent flavor and aroma
Average days to germinate	5 to 7 days
Average days to harvest (after germination)	10 to 14 days
Average weight per tray	3 to 5 ounces
Difficulty	Medium to difficult

Growing Tips

- Cilantro seed sold with split seed hulls has a substantially higher germination rate.
- If split seeds are used, the towel method is effective. Seeds that are not split should be covered with soil.

Harvesting Tips

- Before harvesting, take the time to pull off excess seed hulls from the greens. This will save you time when washing.
- Make sure and allow to grow to the true leaf stage.

Washing Tips

- Generally easy to wash, requiring only one or two rinses.
- Watch out for large seed hulls that tend to remain attached to the tips of the greens.
- Be careful not to overdry.

Possible Challenges

- If using whole seeds, it can be difficult to obtain dense germination and good yields.

Our Thoughts

Micro cilantro is a beautiful, unique microgreen popular with chefs. It boasts such strong aroma that it can overwhelm other flavors. We recommend using it alone versus adding it to a mix. Although sometimes difficult to grow and achieve good yields, it makes a nice specialty microgreen to offer. Finding a source of split cilantro seeds can help you achieve success with this crop.

Brief History

Cilantro, also known as coriander, is one of the world's oldest spices. Spanning from 5000 BC to modern times, it has been used medicinally and culinarily around the world. It is thought to be native to Southern Europe but has been known in Asia for thousands of years. China, India, Egypt, Greece, and Rome all used it in ancient times for both its seed and leaf. This strong herb has been used to ease labor pains as well as to reduce flatulence. Many cultures believe it to be an aphrodisiac and, if taken in large doses, it can even act as a narcotic. It is also very effective in the chelation of heavy metals out of the body. Some records report cilantro making its way to the North American colonies by the late seventeenth century.

(Garden) Cress

Family	Brassicaceae
Genus and species	*Lepidium sativum*
Varieties we recommend	Presto, Cressida (Curly)
Taste	Tangy, very spicy
Average days to germinate	2 to 3 days
Average days to harvest (after germination)	8 to 10 days
Average weight per tray	3 to 5 ounces
Difficulty	Medium

Growing Tips

- Cress has a mucilaginous seed. This makes the towel method especially useful for pulling off seed hulls and avoiding excess soil when washing.
- Fairly lightweight; sow thickly for bigger yields.
- If the towel is removed early in the germination process, you will pull out much of the still-germinating seed. Wait another day to remove the towel until roots have set.

Harvesting Tips

- The stems and cotyledons of cress break easily, so be gentle when harvesting.
- Be aware of soil clumping on the base of the stem. When harvesting, simply cut high enough to avoid it.

Washing Tips

- Can be quick to wash if towel method is used, usually requiring one to two rinses.
- If soil is used to cover the cress seed, you will find dirt and seed hulls stuck to the greens. This makes washing very time consuming and requires several rinses even when using the two-stage washing method.

Possible Challenges

- Slow and tedious to wash if soil is used to cover.
- Will start to yellow and rot if it continues to grow past its peak.
- Is easily overdried. Be mindful to fluff often if using a fan to dry. Fluff by gently turning the greens so that what was on the bottom gets put on top and what was on the top gets put on the bottom.
- Due to its delicate nature, cress has a short shelf life. Use an airtight bag or container when storing to avoid rapid degradation.

Our Thoughts

This little green packs a lot of spice for its size. It is delicious in salad dressings and adds flair to wraps and sandwiches. Although it can be challenging to keep it looking fresh and vibrant when storing, it makes a nice addition to the home grower's pallet. Avoid adding it to a mix as it may degrade faster than your other ingredients.

Brief History

Garden cress, also referred to as peppercress, is related to both common watercress and mustard. As evident from its name, it has a strong peppery flavor, making it popular as a fresh addition to sandwiches and salads. The lineage of garden cress has been identified by the variety of languages in which it is described. Records date its early use back to 400 BC by the Persians. Along with helping with digestive and parasitic issues, peppercress has a host of other medicinal properties. It is known to both repel insects and help with insect bites. Its stimulating qualities have made it known for being an appetite stimulant and aphrodisiac. Other health claims range from stopping hair loss to protecting against leprosy. Cress enjoyed a royal stature in the middle ages, prepared with bread and eaten in salads. Garden cress was brought to the Americas by the late sixteenth century.

Endive

Family	Asteraceae
Genus and species	*Cichorium endivia*
Varieties we recommend	Bianca Riccia, Ruffea
Taste	Pleasantly bitter
Average days to germinate	3 to 5 days
Average days to harvest (after germination)	8 to 12 days
Average weight per tray	3 to 5 ounces
Difficulty	Medium

Growing Tips

- Can germinate and grow in cold conditions.
- Oversowing can lead to stunted growth.
- Can be pH sensitive, so try to keep it under 7.

Harvesting Tips

- Endive doesn't produce a long stem like most other seedlings but instead stays short and wide, so you will want to harvest close to the soil.
- Due to how closely endive grows to the soil, it's easy to catch a lot of dirt with your greens during harvest. To avoid this, use a smaller pair of scissors and take your time harvesting.

Washing Tips

- Generally, this is a crop you will want to take your time with. It often takes at least two washes to get clean.
- If using in a mix, wash separately.

Possible Challenges

- In the heat of the summer, endive leaves can burn if left in the midday sun. To avoid burning, do not water midday and keep your greens out of direct sunlight when the sun is at its strongest.
- Birds love this seed. If our endive trays are not covered with lids, even in the greenhouse, our local songbirds will peel back the paper towels and devour all the germinating seed. (They seem to be connoisseurs of the endive seed in particular and don't bother with our other seed varieties.)
- Endive's growth can be affected by your water's pH, so it helps to keep it under 7.

Our Thoughts

Endive can provide interesting variation in any micro mix. Its unique leaf shape and bold bitter flavor create varying texture and contrast. Its cotyledons and true leaves look similar to lettuce, but endive is much hardier as a microgreen.

Brief History

Endive, escarole, and chicory are all names for this bitter, nutritious salad green. Like many vegetables, it was originally found growing wild and was used medicinally. The Egyptians, Greeks, and Romans all recognized endive for its stimulating effect on the liver. It has also been said to be an effective sedative and appetite stimulant. Its unique flavor was a catalyst for its early cultivation, which began in the mid-sixteenth century in England. While it is unclear when endive began being cultivated in the United States, there are records of some form of endive growing in United States gardens by the early nineteenth century. Today there are several varieties being cultivated. Many growers choose to blanch this plant for a few weeks before harvesting. This creates a "whitening" of its heart that lends a more tender texture and less bitter taste. Other types of endive, such as Bianca Riccia, are often grown as a "cut-and-come-again" salad ingredient and have a bright yellow curly leaf with a mildly bitter flavor.

Mustard

Family	Brassicaceae
Genus and species	*Brassica juncea*
Varieties we recommend	Red Giant, Ruby Streaks, Garnet Red
Taste	Mildly spicy
Average days to germinate	3 to 4 days
Average days to harvest (after germination)	6 to 10 days
Average weight per tray	Red Giant and Garnet Red, 4 to 6 ounces, Ruby Streaks and Crimson Tide, 4 to 8 ounces
Difficulty	Easy

Growing Tips

- Easy to obtain true leaves.
- Cold weather hardy.

Harvesting Tips

- To showcase the color of the cotyledons, you will want to cut high on their white stems.
- Fast and easy to harvest.

Washing Tips

- Mustard's many small seed hulls tend to collect on the edges of your tub.
- One wash is usually sufficient.

Possible Challenges

- Mustard's cotelydons can yellow if allowed to grow for too long.

Our Thoughts

The greens of the mustard family are colorful, hearty, and easy to grow. Mustard is a great addition to any Asian mix. Its dependability in germination and yield make it an asset to any growing repertoire. There are many varieties of mustard to choose from and each look distinct. Mizuna, Crimson Tide, and Ruby Streaks all offer a tooth-shaped leaf with varying colors. Garnet Red and Red Giant have a rounded leaf with deep contrasting colors. Mustards range from green to deep purple, making them a very diverse crop. They are very tasty, offering mild to spicy flavor.

Brief History

Known for its fiery nature, mustard dates back five thousand years. It is one of the few plants that have been cultivated for both its seed and leaf. Mustard as a condiment evolved from a paste created by the Greeks. Along with its intense flavor, mustard also yields medicinal benefits. It was said to help with the sting of a scorpion as well as to serve as a poultice for various ailments. The leaf of the mustard has been used everywhere in cooking, from China to the United States, and it remains popular for its flavor and nutritional value. Mustard isn't exempt from its own lore. It was said to give a German bride power in her household if sewn into the hem of her wedding dress and thought to provide protection from evil spirits.

Pac Choi

Family	Brassicaceae
Genus and species	*Brassica rapa*
Varieties we recommend	Kinkoh (Yellow), Red Choi
Taste	Sweet full flavor
Average days to germinate	3 to 4 days
Average days to harvest (after germination)	7 to 10 days
Average weight per tray	8 to 10 ounces
Difficulty	Easy

Growing Tips

- Like all of the Asian greens we have experimented with, we have found pac choi to be both hardy and easy to grow.
- The more direct sunlight it receives, the deeper its red color (when growng red pac choi).

Harvesting Tips

- Harvest an inch above the soil.
- Gives heavy yields and is quick to harvest.

Washing Tips

- Washing is quick and easy.
- The small black seeds are easy to see and remove.
- One rinse is usually sufficient.

Possible Challenges

- None that we have found.

Our Thoughts

We are happy to have an array of Asian greens available to us. They never disappoint and yield sturdy, strong greens with heavy weights and good structure. They can be sown densely and look beautiful with or without their true leaf. A red variety is available that has a variegated green and red leaf. Red pac choi is a crop that benefits from the cold. Its cotyledons and true leaves transform from a light smoky purple to a deep maroon in the colder months. If growing pac choi inside, you may want to expose it to the colder outside air a day or two before you harvest to simulate the change in weather. Kinkoh pac choi is similar to Tokyo Bekana and features a brilliant yellow cotyledon and rounded leaf. It also boasts a sweet taste that makes it great as a base of a mix.

Brief History

Common names for pac choi are bok choy and Chinese cabbage. It has also been described as Chinese chard, Chinese mustard, and celery mustard. Although both are identified as *Brassica rapa,* it is distinctly different from its close relative napa cabbage. Native to China, records date its use in cooking back over six thousand years. While early cultivation confined it chiefly to Asia, pac choi is now used and available all over the world.

Pea

Family	Leguminosae (Fabaceae)
Genus and species	*Pisum sativum*
Varieties we recommend	Dwarf Sugar Grey
Taste	Sweet fresh pea flavor
Average days to germinate	3 to 5 days
Average days to harvest (after germination)	5 to 7 days
Average weight per tray	8 to 12 ounces
Difficulty	Easy

Growing Tips

- Easy to grow.
- Cover seeds with soil, making sure they do not become exposed once watered.
- Pea is a cool-weather crop. In spring and fall, tendrils will be sweet, small, and compact (3 to 4 inches).
- If grown in the summer, be sure to keep them in the shade. Without shade, pea shoots can lose their dark color and sweet flavor.
- Sprouted pea seeds make a tasty treat for critters. If growing them outside, keep them covered and off the ground.

Harvesting Tips

- Very easy to harvest.
- If allowed to grow too large, cut high on the stem.

Washing Tips

- One quick rinse is sufficient.
- Pea tendrils tend to repel water, making them quick to dry.

Possible Challenges

- A favorite with the rodents.
- Summer heat can effect growth and flavor.

Our Thoughts

Whether growing for the home or to sell, pea shoots are an excellent crop. Easy to harvest and process, they make a great addition to any salad and make a beautiful garnish. Their fresh spring taste is a treat in the winter months. Peas prefer a cooler climate, making them lose some of their sweetness in the summer.

Brief History

Peas have a vast and varied history. For such a small vegetable, they have made quite an impact on the world. According to Norse mythology, Thor sent dragons to fill the village wells with peas as a punishment. The dragons, being sloppy in their task, dropped peas onto the soil, which then germinated and grew. To honor (and not upset) Thor, the Norse people cultivated the peas and ate them only on Thor's day (Thursday). Peas made their way though French and British cooking and played a key role in sustaining nutrition in colonial times in the United States. They bridged the gap between rich and poor. Canned, frozen, or fresh, peas continue to be a part of the American diet.

Radish

Family	Brassicaceae
Genus and species	*Raphanus sativus*
Varieties we recommend	Hong Vit, China Rose
Taste	Potent spicy flavor
Average days to germinate	3 to 4 days
Average days to harvest (after germination)	6 to 8 days
Average weight per tray	8 to 10 ounces
Difficulty	Easy

Growing Tips

- Just as radishes are known for how easily and quickly they grow in the garden, micro radishes are no exception.
- They do not require any special attention and always perform.
- Radish's large seeds can be covered with soil or towels.

Harvesting Tips

- If harvested at the optimal time, they will remain tender and keep their vibrant stem color.
- If they are allowed to grow past their prime, they will become woody and tough with oversized cotyledons.
- Harvest low on the stem to feature its beautiful color.

Washing Tips

- Generally easy to wash.
- Occasionally you may notice that some of the leaves have black spots on them. This is something to look out for in the washing process.

- You will find an abundance of seed hulls in your wash water with this crop. They are large and light and will float to the top of your tub. Simply use your hand to skim the surface and remove them. Repeat this step until all of the seed hulls are removed. The two-stage washing method can be helpful if you find that seed hulls are hiding under the leaves.

Possible Challenges

- If grown in shade, Hong Vit's signature purple stem can lose its deep color. Full sun will help achieve optimal stem color. Exposing radish to colder temperatures will also help with this.
- China Rose seed quality can vary greatly. We have grown seeds that produced anywhere from white to rich pink stems. While full sun and cold stress will help with its color, some seeds don't seem to be able to make nice pink stems.
- Lower-quality China Rose seed will produce an abundance of black spots on its cotyledons.

Our Thoughts

Hong Vit radish is a favorite. We have found that the stunning contrast of its dark green cotyledons to its vibrant purple stem to be both beautiful as a single crop or as a splash of color and spice to any mix.

Brief History

Radish is perhaps most well known today for how easy it is to grow. Because the radish is quick to germinate and fast to fruit, beginner gardeners have little trouble adding it to their growing repertoire. While the radish's exact origin is disputed, the Chinese have been growing it for thousands of years. The Egyptians integrated radishes into their diet and enjoyed them early in their civilization. While we are used to small red beauties, old European varieties ranged from white to red and have been recorded to weigh as much as one hundred pounds. Radishes were one of the earlier crops cultivated by settlers in North America, recorded to have been growing by the mid-seventeenth century.

Tokyo Bekana

Family	Brassicaceae
Genus and species	*Brassica rapa* (*chinensis* group)
Varieties we recommend	Tokyo Bekana
Taste	Sweet lettuce flavor
Average days to germinate	3 to 4 days
Average days to harvest (after germination)	7 to 10 days
Average weight per tray	8 to 10 ounces
Difficulty	Easy

Growing Tips

- Tokyo Bekana is a hardy Asian green.
- It is beautiful at its cotyledon stage but also produces an attractive true leaf.
- Puts on true leaves quickly.

Harvesting Tips

- Harvest an inch above the soil.
- Gives heavy yields and is quick to harvest.

Washing Tips

- Washing is easy with this crop and one rinse is usually sufficient.
- Its small, dark seed hulls contrast with the yellow cotyledons, making them easy to see and remove.

Possible Challenges

- During the summer months, Tokyo's bright yellow turns to a light green.
- Growth can be uneven.

Our Thoughts

This Asian green is easy to grow and produces a dense tray of bright cotyledons. It is reliable and consistent, making it a great base for mixes. We are always looking for a contrasting vivid yellow for the various mixes that we offer our chefs and have been very happy with Tokyo Bekana. Its sweet flavor complements any spicy or bitter flavors you might add to a mix. As this seed can be extremely expensive, take the time to research before purchasing.

Brief History

Tokyo Bekana shares a very similar history with pac choi. Both varieties are thought to have been cultivated for over six thousand years, originating in Asia. Tokyo Bekana is a Chinese cabbage adapted and bred by the Japanese. It carries similar characteristics to a napa cabbage but features a light yellow leaf and more delicate texture. Perhaps the specific cultivation of Tokyo Bekana, also called *pei tsai,* began after the parent species, *Brassica rapa,* was brought from China back to Japan after soldiers returned from the Russo-Japanese War.

COMPOSTING

After you have cut your tray of greens, you will be left with a flat of soil, full of fibrous stems and roots. Since you have cut your greens below their cotyledons, they will not grow for a second time. However, taking your trays of used earth and transforming them into a rich soil is very easy.

Vegetables grown on farms and in gardens can be classified by how heavily they feed on the soil. Unlike vegetables that are growing in the soil for long periods of time, micro-greens are growing for only a week or two. This short cycle results in little taxation of the nutrients in the soil. Even though your soil has been used once for growing microgreens, it is still alive with biological life, organic matter, trace minerals, and nutrients. After being amended and composted, it can be used to jumpstart a small garden plot or to grow another crop of greens.

If you are unable due to space or time, or not interested in composting, there are several options for spreading the wealth of your soil. If you live in an urban area, seek out a com-munity garden. Store your soil in five-gallon buckets or trash bags and deliver it to the garden once a week. Other options include friends' and neighbors' gardens or a local school doing a garden project with their students. Another possibility that is less involved than creating a compost heap is filling a few large flower pots with your used soil. Sprinkle a layer of alfalfa or kelp (both of which can be purchased at any local nursery) and layer in your soil. Keep-ing it moist, let it break down for a few weeks to a couple of months, depending on weather conditions. When you notice that the roots have incorporated into the soil, plant a flower, vegetable, or kitchen herb in the pot!

With so many methods of composting out there, the idea of making your own compost can seem daunting. With our busy lives, it may seem like just one more thing to do. In this chapter, we will show you how composting can be easy, quick, and even enjoyable. Composting can be especially fun and educational for young children. Being a part of the transformation of soil is both rewarding and fascinating. This is another area in which experimenting is definitely encouraged. Don't let someone tell you there is only one way to make great compost. Following a few simple guidelines will allow you to integrate compost-ing into your life with ease. The ultimate form of recycling, composting allows you to trans-form your kitchen scraps, yard waste, and used microgreen trays into rich, healthy soil.

The compost pile is an asset to any home or garden. It is basically a layered heap made up of just about any available organic material, such as grass clippings, leaves, hay, straw, kitchen scraps, harvested microgreen trays, and even paper towels. Creating a compost pile allows you to evenly break down these materials into rich, dark soil that is teeming with biological life.

If you were to let any organic material sit around for long enough outside, it would eventually break down and become soil. Just look to the forest and you can see this happening every day. After trees drop their leaves, the leaves slowly break down to become the soil that then enriches the trees themselves; even a fallen tree will eventually do the same.

In nature, the process of decaying happens due to the activity of microbial life. From worms to bacteria and fungi, the soil is so full of life that it is hard to truly comprehend. It has been said that there is more life in a spoonful of healthy soil than humans currently living on the planet. Depending on its fertility, the number of microbes in a tablespoon of soil varies from millions to billions. If the conditions in a compost heap are ideal, their numbers are unimaginable. Like you and me, biological life needs air, moisture, food, and warmth to thrive.

Air

As the microbes are digesting the components of your compost pile, they are also consuming oxygen. When building your pile, it is helpful to layer in coarse material, such as leaves, straw, hay, etc. This creates pockets of air that increase circulation and allow for faster decomposition. After a few weeks you will notice your heap will start to shrink as the microbes use up the available oxygen. To keep the digestion of the pile on track, you will want to turn it regularly. If you find that you do not have a supply of coarse material available, turning your pile more frequently can be helpful.

Moisture

When trying to obtain the proper moisture in your pile, imagine a rung-out sponge. If you were to squeeze a handful of your compost, you should get only one or two drops of water. The key here is for the pile to feel moist, not wet. Saturated soil reduces the amount of air available to the microbes. Each time you add new material to your pile, gently and evenly water it. This will help maintain proper moisture throughout the pile. If the pile gets too wet or too dry, composting will slow. If this happens, turn your pile and make adjustments. We've always thought of turning our compost as a reset button for the composting process. You can always add more dry material or water, if needed, and try again.

Food

The two types of "food" that make up a balanced compost pile can be referred to as either nitrogenous or carbonaceous. Materials such as kitchen scraps, manure, and coffee grounds are nitrogen rich. Materials such as leaves, straw, and shredded newspaper are carbon rich. Think of your nitrogen materials as being fresh, green, or wet and your carbon materials as brown, woody, or dry. Fresh green hay would be considered a nitrogen food, but the same hay, if allowed to dry out and turn brown, would be considered more carbonaceous. The trick with these two foods is the ratio in your pile. You will always want quite a bit more carbon than nitrogen, thirty parts of carbon to every one part of nitrogen. Anything you add to your pile has its own C:N ratio. Below is a chart showing some of the more common ingredients you might use. Above all else, realize that you can't go wrong. Remember, the fallen tree in the forest will eventually turn back into soil.

Carbon to Nitrogen Ratio Chart	
Sawdust*	300:1 to 500:1
Newspaper	170:1
Paper towels	120:1
Straw	80:1
Leaves	60:1
Kitchen scraps	20:1
Grass clippings	20:1
Coffee grounds	20:1

*Depending on its stage of decomposition.

Warmth

Heat is a good indicator of how balanced all of the other factors (food, air, moisture) are in your pile. The layers of soil in the pile have inoculated it with a population of microbes. The closer your carbon-nitrogen ratio is to 30:1, the quicker the microbes will start to thrive and consume your materials. The warmth the pile generates is actually due to the metabolic activity of the microbes. In a compost pile there is usually a domino effect: the cool-loving microbes start the party, generate enough heat for the warm-loving microbes to take over, and they, in turn, generate enough warmth for the heat-loving microbes to take over.

To check the warmth of your pile, simply put your hand inside, 8 to 12 inches towards the center. If your pile has started to heat, soil in the center will be warm, even hot to the touch. To get a more accurate reading, use a thermometer. Large weather-resistant compost thermometers are easily found at any gardening store. To ensure any weed seeds are killed off and to reduce the time it takes to make finished compost, you may want to get your pile up to 150 to 160 degrees F for a short period. For most people, though, having a pile that generates a bit of warmth is perfect. It may take a little more time to compost, but it's not a race to see who finishes first.

Making a Compost Pile

When building your pile, think of a layered cake. The spongy cake layer will consist of your carbon ingredients, and the layers of frosting will be your nitrogen ingredients. Once you have gathered your materials, you will want to start layering them. Your pile size should be at least 3 x 3 x 3 feet but can be as large as space and materials will allow. Keep the size convenient to turn and work with. The first layer of your heap should be your carbonaceous material (i.e., straw, leaves, etc.). The reason for starting with these materials is to help with proper drainage and air circulation. Shoot for around 6 to 8 inches for this layer to have a solid start. The next layer will be composed of your nitrogenous material. If using wet kitchen scraps, a couple of inches will be sufficient. If either lawn clippings or fresh (undried) hay are available, you will want to add a slightly thicker layer. If you choose to include additional amendments, you can layer them in now.

Avoid using meats and fats as they will tend to attract hungry animals and break down

slower than your other ingredients. If you choose to add eggshells to your pile, take the time to crush them up. You may still notice small pieces of eggshell in your finished compost. Don't be alarmed, as this is purely an aesthetic issue. They will continue to be digested in the soil. To avoid this uneven decomposition, simply bake your eggshells in the oven at 400 degrees F for 15 to 20 minutes. Baking the moisture out of the shells will allow them to be pulverized into a powder. This extra step will let the shells be digested by the compost pile more quickly.

The next layer will be composed of an inch of soil, potting soil, or compost (whichever is available to you). Now would be a good time to layer in your used trays of soil from your harvested microgreens. The purpose of this layer is to inoculate your pile with microbes; the richer the soil, the better. It is a good idea to water your layers as you go. After you have finished all of your first layers, you will now want to begin again with your carbon-rich material and repeat the process until you have run out of your ingredients or reached your ideal size.

Another way of recycling harvested trays is to create a pile made solely of the used microgreen soil. This is a good option for people who don't have other materials they want to compost. The microbial life will quickly break down the roots and stems in the soil so it can be reintegrated back into growing. As you are layering your flats of soil, it helps to add a dusting of alfalfa meal and/or water the pile with a bit of liquid kelp. This helps to restore any trace minerals that the soil has lost. Crab meal can also be sprinkled in, as it is a gentle source of nitrogen and calcium.

If using potting soil that has been sterilized, you will want to inoculate your pile with a dose of beneficial microbes. This can be achieved in a couple of different ways. You can use a compost accelerator or microbial inoculant powder. Both of which can be used dry and layered into a pile. They are found at most gardening stores or at Johnny's Selected Seeds (www.johnnyseeds. com.). You can also make a compost or vermicompost tea. To do this you will need a small aquarium air pump, a bucket, compost or worm castings, and molasses or fruit juice of some kind. Fill your bucket with water; add a few large handfuls of compost and a "sip" of juice or molasses. Use the air pump to keep the tea bubbling for a day or two, and then water your pile with it.

Additional Amendments for Your Compost Pile

Agricultural Lime (such as dolomite): Available at any local garden store, lime is a good source of calcium and magnesium. Whether or not it is necessary to use lime depends on the volume of acidic materials you use (i.e., fruits, coffee grounds, tomatoes, pine needles, etc.). In acidic conditions, a light dusting helps to promote digestion of your compost-pile ingredients and prevents souring. As over-liming can cause nitrogen loss, add only a very light dusting directly on your acidic materials. The lime should be applied lightly enough to see the materials below versus having a solid white layer. Ground oyster shells can also be used with similar effect.

Alfalfa Meal: Alfalfa is an extraordinary plant. Its ability to send roots 40 to 60 feet deep in the earth and bring up trace elements and minerals that other plants can't reach makes it a great resource. Made up of ground alfalfa, its meal is a great addition to any soil or compost pile. When adding it to your pile, put a thick dusting after the soil layer.

Other Meals (Blood, Crab, Fish, and Feather): If you have an abundance of carbonaceous material and need more nitrogenous material for your pile, you could always supplement with a bit of one of these meals. Aside from crab, they are all extremely high in nitrogen, so you will want to use them sparingly. A gentler form of nitrogen, our personal favorite, is crab meal. Crabs (as well as other crustaceans) have a substance in their shells called chitin. When chitin is introduced into the soil, it stimulates a population of chitin-loving microbes. After eating all of the chitin available in the crab meal, these microbes turn their attention to the nematodes in the soil, which are also made up of chitin. This cycle helps to balance the overabundance of parasitic nematodes.

Liquid Seaweed/Kelp: For thousands of years the sea has been a treasure trove for our farms and gardens. Available in abundance, seaweed is one of the ocean's jewels. Kelp, in particular, is a variety of seaweed that is extremely high in minerals, vitamins, and trace elements.

If you live in a coastal area and have access to seaweed, it makes a great raw layer in your compost pile. Treat it as you would wet kitchen scraps, layering in around two inches. If seaweed is not available to you in its raw form, liquid kelp is the next best alternative. You can have a watering can ready with just a couple tablespoons of kelp mixed in the water. An alternative is buying a dispenser that would attach between your faucet and hose. This device allows you to drip in an adjustable amount of liquid every time you use your hose. This second option is slightly more expensive but is convenient if you also want to fertilize your garden or other outdoor plants. There are plenty of liquid amendments available at local gardening stores or online. With so many brands and claims, just be sure to choose a product with pure ingredients and nutrient-rich kelp over green seaweed.

Compost Receptacles

Most compost bins are medium-sized four walled containers made of plastic or wood. The average bin is between 3 and 4 feet wide and tall. Using this type of compost receptacle allows you to retain the shape and structure of your compost pile, keeping it neat and well kept. Another advantage of using this type of vessel is that it is easily covered, providing protection from excess moisture and heat. As you acquire materials for your compost pile, such as kitchen scraps and lawn clippings, this type of compost vessel allows you to layer as you go. To speed up the composting process, simply lift and move your bin to the area adjacent and take your now-exposed pile and shovel it back into the bin, taking what was on top and making it now the bottom, and what was on the bottom, on top. This is a simple, fast, and easy way to turn your pile. Turning a compost pile gives you a window into its progress, creates necessary aeration, and speeds up the composting process.

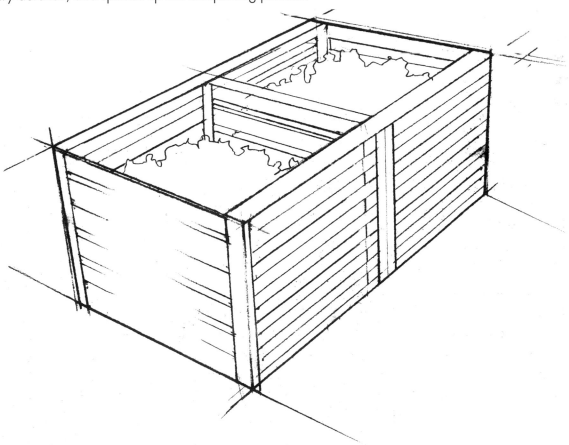

Tumbler

A tumbler is basically a barrel commonly made of plastic that stands suspended on its side or straight up. These composters have a door on their side or a screw-off top that can be opened to feed your materials. It is designed to make turning and aerating your compost quick and easy, thus enabling you to maintain "hot composting" conditions. Tumblers range in size from 1 cubic foot all the way up to 25 cubic feet. The cost ranges from $120 to $600.

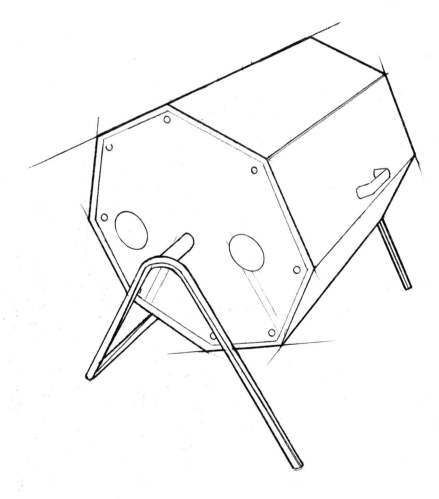

Vermiculture

Vermiculture is another exciting option that you can integrate into your composting process. In healthy soil on a farm or garden, worms are consuming vast amounts of decaying organic matter. The life of a worm basically involves eating and excreting. As they are eating, they are breaking down plant material and excreting it out. Their droppings are your gold. Worm castings are a huge asset to healthy soil and therefore healthy greens. They are a perfectly balanced food for plants and microbes.

Vermiculture is the concentrated use of worms in breaking down your plant matter (i.e., kitchen scraps, coffee grounds) to create dark vital soil. Getting started with worms is quite easy. You will first need to give your worms a home commonly called a worm bin. There are countless systems varying in price and size that can all be purchased online and sent to you by mail, or it's always worth checking to see if there are any stores selling systems locally. You can also easily construct your own. You will find many do-it-yourself guides online to help you with this. If you receive your supplies by mail, you will have a box of worms waiting in your mailbox or at the post office, so be sure to check your mail regularly after you order!

Once you have chosen or created your worm receptacle, you must make sure your worms are well fed and have adequate bedding. We have found that kitchen scraps and used microgreen soil make a great blend. Your kitchen scraps and root matter will provide their food while your soil will buffer them

from excess moisture, heat, and cold. If you keep their environment ideal, your worms will thrive and multiply.

One important note to make is that you do not want to create a compost pile in your worm bin. As we said earlier, when making a compost pile, you want to create conditions that allow it to heat up. These same conditions will kill your worms! Worms like things cool. Temperatures between 55 and 75 degrees F seem to be ideal. To avoid heating up your worm bin, be moderate when adding carbon. We once made the mistake of adding too much leftover pasta to ours. This resulted in the bin getting so hot over the next day that we lost most of our worms. Even after removing the pasta, it still took several days for the bin to cool back down.

Creating your "worm farm" can also be a fun project to start with children. It is another hands-on opportunity to teach them about nature and its life cycles. Being able to watch, over a period of time, as your scraps are eaten and transformed is fascinating. We have been very impressed by the quality and quantity of worm castings that our system easily produces. Integrating vermiculture has been a huge asset to our operation and has increased the fertility of our soil exponentially.

RECIPES:
FOOD AS ART

There is something fundamentally uplifting about every aspect of food. The nourishment we receive from it goes back to our first moments as a newborn. The connection between mother and child through food is something only the best poet or painter could come close to depicting. Our memories of fresh-baked cookies from our grandmothers or Thanksgiving dinner with our families invoke a powerful sense of well-being. Even popcorn at the movies or hot dogs at the ball game become fond childhood memories.

The ability of food to deepen and transform a moment is carried on as we grow. Food not only provides physical nourishment but can also offer an opportunity to build community and friendship and strengthen families. Sitting amongst others surrounded by good food, laughter, and conversation allows us to slow down and celebrate life. It has been said that feasting is the opposite of war.

For some, the reverence of food starts before the feast with its preparation. In a way, this too can be a feast of the senses with the coming together of friends, the sharing of recipes and stories, the rhythmical washing, chopping, and stirring of the food, and the sweet smells that are slowly released.

This chapter will give you some fun ideas for incorporating microgreens into your cooking. From entrées to desserts, microgreens can add flavor, nutrition, and beauty to your dishes. We have asked a few Big Sur chefs to offer their favorite ways to use microgreens. Recipes range from a sweet take on basil to a broccoli medley. We have also included a simple salad that we enjoy as well as some ideas for exciting mixes.

Remember, the possibilities are truly endless and experimentation is the key to discovering new flavors.

Metric Conversion Chart

Liquid and Dry Measures		
U.S.	Canadian	Australian
¼ teaspoon	1 mL	1 ml
½ teaspoon	2 mL	2 ml
1 teaspoon	5 mL	5 ml
1 tablespoon	15 mL	20 ml
¼ cup	50 mL	60 ml
⅓ cup	75 mL	80 ml
½ cup	125 mL	125 ml
⅔ cup	150 mL	170 ml
¾ cup	175 mL	190 ml
1 cup	250 mL	250 ml
1 quart	1 liter	1 litre

Temperature Conversion Chart	
Fahrenheit	Celsius
250	120
275	140
300	150
325	160
350	180
375	190
400	200
425	220
450	230
475	240
500	260

Recipes from
Chef Craig von Foerster
Sierra Mar Restaurant at the Post Ranch Inn

Broccoli Tasting

Serves 8

Pâté Brisée

3 cups flour

1 tablespoon baking powder

2 teaspoons salt

1 teaspoon sugar

$1/2$ pound very cold unsalted butter, cut into small cubes

$3/4$ cup milk

Tart

3 bunches broccoli

Pâté Brisée (recipe above)

3 eggs

1 cup half-and-half

$1/2$ cup grated white cheddar cheese

$1 1/2$ teaspoons salt

$1/4$ teaspoon cayenne pepper

Soup

1 leek, julienned (light part only)

1 tablespoon butter

1 clove garlic, chopped

1 cup vegetable or chicken broth

$1/2$ cup reserved blanched broccoli florets

2 tablespoons crème fraîche

Salt and white pepper to taste

Red Wine Vinaigrette

2 tablespoons good-quality red wine vinegar

1 teaspoon water

1/4 teaspoon Dijon mustard

2 teaspoons diced shallots

1/4 teaspoon salt

6 tablespoons extra virgin olive oil

1/8 teaspoon freshly ground black pepper

Salad

3 pieces reserved broccoli stems

Micro broccoli

Salt and pepper to taste

3 tablespoons Red Wine Vinaigrette (recipe above)

To make the Pâté Brisée

1. Mix the flour, baking powder, salt, and sugar in the bowl of a stand mixer fitted with a paddle attachment. Run on low for a few seconds to mix.
2. Add the cold butter and run on low speed for 5 minutes or until the pieces of butter are pea sized.
3. Add the milk and mix just until the dough comes together.
4. Turn out the dough and knead for a few seconds until the dough comes together. Wrap in plastic and refrigerate for 1 hour.

NOTE: *This recipe will make more than you will need. Wrap the extra tightly and freeze for up to 1 month.*

To make the tart

1. Preheat oven to 350 degrees F.
2. Bring a gallon of lightly salted water to a boil and have an ice-water bath ready. Trim off the tops of the broccoli and cut into florets. Reserve the stems for the salad. Blanch the florets in the boiling water until crisp-tender, about 2 minutes, and transfer to the ice bath.
3. Lightly flour a work surface and roll out the Pâté Brisée to 1/8 inch thick and then cut into 2 (6-inch) circles. Lay each circle over a tart mold and press dough down to fit in the mold. Trim off the overlapping dough with a sharp knife.

4. Fill the tart shells with pie weights and blind bake for 8 minutes in the preheated oven.
5. Drain and chop the broccoli florets, reserving $1/2$ cup for the soup.
6. Whisk the eggs together with the half-and-half, cheese, salt, and cayenne pepper; fold in the chopped broccoli and fill each tart shell.
7. Bake 20 minutes or until custard is set. To test, gently shake the tart and see if the filling jiggles. If it is not set, return to the oven for a few minutes more.

To make the soup

1. Clean the leek by removing the green top and outer layer. Cut in half lengthwise and julienne. Place in a bowl of cold water and gently swish around to loosen any dirt. Let sit for a few minutes to allow any dirt to settle to the bottom of the bowl, and then gently scoop the leeks off the top and drain.
2. Melt the butter in a 4-quart pot. Add the leeks and garlic and sweat over medium heat. Do not allow to brown. When the leeks are soft, add the stock and simmer for 15 minutes.
3. Place $1/2$ cup of the reserved blanched broccoli in the container of a blender, pour the hot liquid over the top, and carefully blend until smooth. Transfer to a small pot and whisk in the crème fraîche. Season with salt and pepper to taste and keep warm.

To make the vinaigrette

1. Place the vinegar, water, mustard, shallots, and salt in a bowl and let sit for 5 minutes.
2. Add the oil in a slow, steady stream while whisking constantly to incorporate. Finish with the black pepper.

To make the salad

1. Peel the broccoli stems down until they are a very pale green (about halfway through). Cut stems on a bias into $1/4$-inch-thick slices and toss with the micro broccoli, salt, pepper, and Red Wine Vinaigrette to taste.

To plate, warm the tart and cut into wedges. Fill a glass with broccoli soup. Place one section of tart on a plate and top with micro broccoli lightly dressed with the vinaigrette. Place the glass of the soup and salad on the plate.

NOTE: *Always dress microgreens lightly and handle gently to avoid making them soggy and heavy. They have an intense flavor that requires very little seasoning.*

Grilled Beef Tataki with Crispy Wonton and Asian Microgreen Salad

Serves 6

Grilled Beef
1 (2-pound) flat-iron steak
4 ounces ginger, sliced and roughly chopped
4 green onions, sliced and roughly chopped
2 tablespoons canola oil
1/2 cup soy sauce
1 tablespoon sesame oil

Sweet Soy
1 (1-inch-square) piece ginger
1/2 cup soy sauce
1/2 cup brown sugar

Oriental Vinaigrette
2 tablespoons soy sauce
2 tablespoons rice wine vinegar
1 teaspoon powdered sugar
2 teaspoons grated ginger
1/4 cup canola oil
1 tablespoon sesame oil

Crispy Wonton
3 quarts oil
1/2 package wonton skins, julienned

Asian Microgreen Salad

3 tablespoons canola oil

2 cups sliced shiitake mushrooms

4 ounces Asian microgreens (varieties and ratios on page 166)

¼ cup Sweet Soy (recipe above)

1 (2.2-ounce) package daikon sprouts or micro daikon

1 ounce micro cilantro

¼ cup Oriental Vinaigrette (recipe on previous page)

To make the beef

1. Toss all the beef ingredients into a bowl and rub into the steak. Let marinate for 1 hour before cooking and work on the rest of the recipe while waiting.
2. Grill the steak over a hot broiler until rare, about 2 minutes per side. Let rest for about 5 minutes.

To make the sweet soy

Place all ingredients in a medium pot and bring to a simmer for 5 minutes, and then strain and chill.

To make the vinaigrette

1. Place the soy sauce, vinegar, powdered sugar, and ginger together in a bowl. Add the oils in a slow, steady stream while whisking constantly to incorporate.
2. Place all ingredients together in a small pot and bring to simmer. Let sit for 5 minutes and strain; set aside.

To make the wontons

1. Heat the oil in a pot large enough to contain the oil when it boils up during frying. Heat the oil to 325 degrees F.
2. Separate wontons into individual strips and fry until golden brown in small batches, about 2 minutes.
3. When the oil stops bubbling, the wontons are done. Transfer to a paper towel–lined plate to drain.

To make the salad

1. Heat the canola oil in a large skillet. Add the mushrooms and sauté until softened and beginning to brown.
2. Add some Sweet Soy and let caramelize on the mushrooms.
3. Transfer mushrooms to plate and let cool. Reserve remaining sweet soy to drizzle over the steak.
4. In a large bowl, toss together the mushrooms with the remaining salad ingredients and the vinaigrette.

To plate, slice the steak into paper-thin slices and fan out on the center of plate. Divide the tossed salad among the plates. Drizzle Sweet Soy over the steak and serve.

Recipes from
Chef Domingo Santamaria
Deetjen's Big Sur Inn

Sesame Encrusted Ahi Tuna with Chilled Asparagus Spears Topped with Micro Radish and Cucumber Salad

Serves 4 to 6

Sesame and Horseradish Vinaigrette
1 medium shallot
$\frac{1}{3}$ cup red wine vinegar
1 cup sesame oil
2 tablespoons fresh horseradish

Chilled Asparagus
Salt
12 to 18 asparagus spears, depending on size

Ahi Tuna
1 ounce caraway
1 ounce coriander
1 ounce sesame seeds
2 pounds ahi tuna
Salt and pepper to taste
Vegetable oil

Cucumber and Micro Radish Salad
2 large cucumbers
3 ounces micro radish (pink-stemmed China Rose or Hong Vit)
Sesame Horseradish Vinaigrette (recipe above)

To make the vinaigrette

1. Chop the shallot into small pieces in a food processor.
2. Slowly add the vinegar.
3. Gradually add the oil to thicken.
4. Finish by shaving fresh horseradish into the food processor. Start with a tablespoon and add more to taste.

NOTE: *If using horseradish from a jar, you may want to add more than if you were using fresh. Fresh horseradish is often much stronger than jarred.*

5. Refrigerate. Will keep for 3 to 4 days.

To make the asparagus

1. Boil 2 quarts of water in a large saucepan. Add salt.
2. Prepare an ice water bath.
3. Put asparagus in boiling water for 40 seconds to 1 minute. Be careful not to overcook or asparagus will become stringy and lose its crisp crunch.

NOTE: *The size of the asparagus will determine the cooking time—small spears 40 seconds; large spears 1 minute.*

4. Quickly remove asparagus from boiling water and place in the ice water bath.
5. Remove asparagus from ice bath and place in a medium bowl; set aside.

To make the Ahi Tuna

1. Preheat oven to 400 degrees F.
2. In a medium sauté pan, combine caraway, coriander, and sesame seeds. Roast in the oven until golden brown, about 5 minutes. Move them around periodically to avoid burning and to ensure even toasting.
3. Remove seeds from oven and let cool. Grind into a powder using a coffee grinder.
4. Cover all sides of tuna with a dusting of the seed powder and season with salt and pepper to taste.
5. Using a medium sauté pan, get the pan very hot and add vegetable oil. Sear tuna for 30 seconds on all sides until golden. Cook medium-rare to medium, depending on your preference.
6. Slice 4 to 5 (1-ounce) pieces for each serving.

To make the salad

1. Shave both skin and meat of cucumber with peeler, making long strings. Set aside several strings to tie around the chilled asparagus.
2. Toss cucumber and micro radish with the Sesame and Horseradish Vinaigrette, reserving a few tablespoons to drizzle over the asparagus.

To plate, drizzle the asparagus with the Sesame and Horseradish Vinaigrette and then wrap groups of 3 or 4 stalks in the reserved cucumber strips. On the plates, fan out medallions of tuna. Top with the Cucumber and Micro Radish Salad and place the cucumber-wrapped asparagus on plate next to tuna. Drizzle with the reserved Sesame and Horseradish Vinaigrette.

Bacon-Wrapped Seared Diver Scallops on Potato and Fennel Salad Topped with Micro Cilantro

Serves 4 to 6

Bacon-Wrapped Scallops

12 to 18 large diver scallops (3 per person)
12 to 18 strips bacon (1 per scallop)
Salt and pepper to taste
2 tablespoons vegetable oil

Chive-and-Yogurt Aioli

3 cloves garlic
6 egg yolks
1 1/2 cups extra virgin olive oil
1/2 cup lemon juice, plus more
Salt and pepper to taste
3 bunches chives
1 to 1 1/2 cups plain yogurt (to taste)

Potato and Fennel Salad

4 small bulbs fennel
3 tablespoons vegetable oil, divided
6 large Yukon Gold potatoes
Salt and pepper to taste
2 tablespoons butter
Chive-and-Yogurt Aioli (recipe above)
Aged balsamic vinegar

Fresh King Crab (optional)
3 medium crab legs
3 cups vegetable stock
2 bay leaves
Tarragon, salt, and pepper to taste

To make the scallops
1. Wrap each scallop in 1 strip bacon.
2. Dust wrapped scallops with salt and pepper.
3. Using a large sauté pan, get the pan very hot and add the vegetable oil. Sear scallops on all sides until the bacon is cooked (scallops will be medium-rare.) If you would like to cook them longer, finish in the oven at 375 to 400 degrees F for 2 to 5 minutes.

To make the aioli
1. Chop garlic into small pieces in a food processor.
2. Slowly add egg yolks into the food processor.
3. Slowly add the oil. If you add the oil too quickly, you will notice the mixture starting to look like mayonnaise. If this happens, stop adding oil and begin adding lemon juice. Add most of the lemon juice until mixture begins to thin out.
4. Add the rest of the oil as aioli starts to thin out.
5. Add salt and pepper and more lemon juice to taste.
6. Chop chives and then throw in the processor. Blend for 30 seconds.
7. Empty contents of food processor into a large mixing bowl. Use a spatula to gradually fold the yogurt into the aioli.
8. Refrigerate. Will keep for 2 to 3 days.

To make the salad
1. Preheat the oven to 375 degrees F.
2. Shave fennel with a mandoline. Sauté in approximately 1 tablespoon vegetable oil until tender.
3. Remove from pan and let cool in a water bath. Fennel tends to turn yellow if not kept in water. It will last at least one day soaking in cold water.

4. Wash potatoes. Toss them whole with salt, pepper, and vegetable oil. Bake on a sheet pan at 375 degrees F until cooked all the way through, about 35 minutes. Remove from oven and let cool.
5. Peel and cut potatoes into small pieces.
6. Mash fennel, potatoes, and butter together. Make sure the ingredients are warm, not hot, so that you don't break the aioli.
7. Stir in Chive-and-Yogurt Aioli to taste, reserving some to drizzle on the plates.

To make the crab (optional)
1. Prepare an ice water bath.
2. Put crabs, vegetable stock, bay leaves, tarragon, salt, and pepper in a large sauté pan.
3. Boil everything together for 3 to 5 minutes.
4. Remove crab and cool in the ice water bath.
5. Shred into small pieces. Add to Potato and Fennel Salad.

To plate, make a bed of Potato and Fennel Salad, and then place scallops on the salad. Top with micro cilantro and drizzle the reserved Chive-and-Yogurt Aioli and aged balsamic vinegar over the entire plate.

Recipes from

Chefs Phil Wojtowicz
and Michelle Rizzolo
Owners and Chefs of The Big Sur Bakery

Microgreen Spring Salad with Carrot Ginger Dressing

Serves 4

Microgreen Spring Salad

2 tablespoons salt
1 handful pea shoot microgreens
$\frac{1}{2}$ cup fava beans, blanched
4 carrots, small diced, blanched
1 handful Tokyo Bekana microgreens
1 handful red pac choi microgreens
1 pinch amaranth microgreens
4 radishes, sliced into thin coins
1 cup peas, blanched
Salt and pepper to taste

Carrot-Ginger Dressing

1 inch ginger, peeled and sliced into coins
$\frac{1}{4}$ cup rice wine vinegar
$\frac{1}{2}$ cup water
1 tablespoon soy sauce
1 tablespoon mayonnaise
Kosher salt and freshly ground black pepper to taste

To make the salad

1. Prepare an ice water bath by filling a large bowl halfway with water and put about 2 dozen ice cubes in it; set aside.
2. Bring a gallon of water to a boil in a large pot. Add salt, and then blanch the peas until they're bright green and tender, about 3 minutes. Immediately remove from the boiling water with a slotted spoon and place in ice water bath to cool for 2 minutes—the ice water will stop the peas from overcooking and help them retain their color. Remove from water bath and set aside.

3. Repeat the blanching process with the fava beans and carrots. Reserve the peas, beans, and $1/2$ cup diced carrot to garnish the salad.
4. Place the microgreens, radishes, carrots, peas, and fava beans in a bowl and season lightly with salt and pepper.

To make the dressing

1. Fill a small pot with cold water. Add the ginger and bring to a rapid boil. Strain out the water and repeat two more times.
2. Place the ginger, $1/2$ cup reserved carrots, rice wine vinegar, and water in a blender and blend until smooth. Remove from the blender and place in a bowl. Whisk in the soy sauce and mayonnaise. Check the seasoning and add salt and pepper if necessary.

To plate, gently toss the salad with just enough dressing to lightly coat the greens and vegetables. Season with salt and pepper to taste. Drizzle some dressing on a platter and place the salad on top.

Roasted Baby Beets with Beet Microgreens and Goat Cheese Crostini

Serves 4

Roasted Beets

24 assorted baby beets, greens reserved

Salt and pepper to taste

$1/4$ cup olive oil, divided

$1/2$ cup water

3 tablespoons red wine vinegar

1 head frisée

2 tablespoons minced chives

2 tablespoons minced scallions

2 ounces beet and/or chard microgreens

Beet Greens

2 tablespoons olive oil

½ small yellow onion, sliced

2 cloves garlic, sliced

Pinch of red chili flakes

2 cups roughly chopped beet greens (reserved from above)

Salt and pepper to taste

1 teaspoon red wine vinegar

Goat Cheese Crostini

4 (½-inch-thick) slices sourdough or country bread

2 tablespoons olive oil

1 tablespoon minced flat-leaf parsley

Salt and pepper to taste

2 to 3 ounces soft goat cheese

To make the beets

1. Trim the stems off the beets. Wash and reserve 2 cups of the greens.
2. Wash the beets, making sure not to puncture the skin. Arrange in a roasting pan in a single layer, season with salt and pepper, and drizzle 2 tablespoons oil and ½ cup water over top. Cover with aluminum foil and roast the beets at 400 degrees F until fork tender, about 35 to 45 minutes, depending on the size of the beets.
3. When the beets are tender, carefully remove them from the roasting pan while still warm, and using a kitchen towel, rub the skin off the beets. Cut beets in half and toss with the vinegar and 2 tablespoons oil.
4. Wash the frisée and remove the green tips from the leaves, leaving only the white and yellow part of the head. Cut the core off and tear the remaining leaves into medium pieces. Put the frisée in a salad bowl and reserve.

To make the greens

1. Heat a large sauté pan over medium heat and drizzle with the oil. Add the onion, garlic, and chili flakes and cook slowly until the onions are translucent, about 4 minutes.
2. Add the reserved greens, season them with salt and pepper, and cook for another 8 to 10 minutes, stirring occasionally, until the stems are tender. Remove from the heat, stir in the vinegar, and transfer to a separate dish to cool; set aside.

To make the crostini

1. Brush both sides of each bread slice with oil and season with parsley, salt, and pepper.
2. Arrange the slices on a sheet pan and place in the oven until lightly toasted, about 7 minutes. Remove the crostini from the oven, spread about 2 tablespoons Beet Greens on each, and top with 1 tablespoon goat cheese. Season with more salt and pepper.
3. Keep the crostini on the sheet pan and warm right before serving.

To plate, reheat the beets over medium-high heat in a sauté pan, and then toss with the frisée, chives, and scallions while still warm. Season with salt and pepper, add remaining beet microgreens, and toss. Transfer to a serving platter. Place warm crostini around the beets.

Buttermilk Panna Cotta with Strawberries and Basil Microgreens

Serves 6

Panna Cotta
1 vanilla bean
1 ¼ cups heavy whipping cream
½ cup sugar
2 tablespoons water
1 ½ teaspoons gelatin
1 ¾ cups buttermilk

Strawberries
1 pint strawberries, quartered
2 tablespoons sugar
¼ cup basil microgreens

Micro Basil Oil
8 ounces micro basil or 3 bunches basil
1 tablespoon salt
1 cup canola oil

To make the panna cotta

1. Split the vanilla bean lengthwise with a paring knife and scrape out the pulp with the back of the knife.
2. Put the pulp and pod into a pot with the cream and sugar. Bring to a boil and steep for 15 minutes.
3. In a bowl, pour in the water and sprinkle with the gelatin. Let sit for 5 minutes until the gelatin expands and resembles applesauce.
4. Bring the cream mixture back to a boil and temper the hot liquid into the gelatin by adding a ladle at a time while whisking vigorously.
5. Remove the vanilla bean pod and stir in the buttermilk. Pour mixture into 6 ramekins and refrigerate until set, at least 4 hours.

To make the strawberries

Right before serving, toss the strawberries with sugar and basil microgreens.

To make the oil

1. Make an ice water bath; set aside.
2. Bring a gallon of water to a boil in a large pot. Add salt and blanch the basil in the boiling water until bright green, about 20 to 30 seconds. Immediately strain the basil and place it in the water bath to cool for 2 minutes—the ice water will stop the basil from over cooking and will help it retain its color.
3. Squeeze the basil dry with a kitchen towel and purée in a blender with the canola oil.
4. Let sit for 2 hours at room temperature and then strain through a fine-mesh sieve. Discard the solids and reserve the basil oil until ready to use.

To plate, unmold the panna cotta and place the ramekin in a glass of hot water for just a few seconds. This will help the panna cotta release from the sides. Flip over into a bowl and garnish with the strawberry and basil salad. Drizzle the Micro Basil Oil over top.

Recipes from
Eric Franks and
Jasmine Richardson
Owners of True Leaf Microgreens

Our Favorite Micro Salad

Serves 4 to 6

8 ounces of your favorite mix of microgreens
2 medium cucumbers
2 avocados
3 tomatoes (optional)
Extra virgin olive oil
Balsamic vinegar
Manchego cheese
Sea salt and freshly ground pepper

1. Make a bed of greens on a large serving platter.
2. Cut cucumbers, avocados, and tomatoes into thin half-moon slices.
3. Lay sliced vegetables over your bed of greens.
4. Dress the salad with a generous amount of olive oil and a dash of balsamic vinegar (using a 3:1 oil to vinegar ratio).
5. Use a grater to cut thin slices of cheese. Arrange cheese on salad. Salt and pepper to taste and then serve.

Microgreen Mixes

Here are a couple of mixes we have had success with. Most of the varieties we call for can be substituted with whatever you are growing. The ratios given create a balanced mix, pairing flavor with appearance. All of these mixes can be used as the base of any favorite salad.

Asian Mix

All of these varieties (besides radish, which becomes tough) are beautiful when grown to their true leaf stage, making this a great microgreen salad mix.

> 3 ½ ounces Tokyo Bekana
> 2 ½ ounces red pac choi
> 1 ½ ounces radish (Hong Vit or China Rose)
> ½ ounce amaranth

Toss all ingredients together and garnish dishes according to your desire.

Micro Mix

This mix is composed of very young micros, harvested at their cotyledon stage. We find that it is better to use as a garnish than as a micro salad.

> 4 ounces purple cabbage
> 2 ounces arugula or broccoli
> 1 ½ ounces endive
> ½ ounce amaranth

Toss all ingredients together and garnish dishes according to your desire.

Spicy Mix

This mix packs some heat. The vibrant colors of the radish and mustard paired with the green arugula and delicate cress make it both beautiful and delicious. Take note that if you are cutting this mix for storage you will want to leave out the cress as it tends to have a shorter shelf life than the other ingredients.

3 ounces radish (Hong Vit or China Rose)
2 ounces mustard
2 ounces arugula
1 ounce (garden) cress

Toss all ingredients together and garnish dishes according to your desire.

Spring Pea Mix

The sweetness of pea shoots, paired with bitter endive and spicy radish, blend nicely for a varied hardy take on a micro salad. Pea shoots make a great base because of their substantial size and mild flavor.

4 ounces pea shoots
2 ounces endive
2 ounces radish (china rose or hong vit)

Toss all ingredients together and garnish dishes according to your desire.

TROUBLESHOOTING

1. What if my seeds aren't germinating?
2. What if my germinating seeds are sticking to the paper towel when I pull it off?
3. What if I see mold when I pull up my towel?
4. What if the seeds come up thickly in some spots and sparsely in others?
5. What if my greens start to rot?
6. What if my tray of soil gets a crack in it?
7. What if my greens are getting tall and weedy?
8. What if my greens are yellowing and stunted?
9. What if the leaves of my greens look burnt?
10. What if my greens become limp after I harvest?

1. What if my seeds aren't germinating?

There are a few simple questions to use as a checklist when encountering this problem:

Seed: Am I using a relatively new, viable seed?

Checking the seed viability is quite easy as long as you know the source of the seed. If you purchased the seed, valuable information will be available to you on the packet. You should be able to find a lot date, ideal temperature range for germination, average percentage of germination, and sometimes days until germination. If you find that your seed has a low germination rate (anything below 80 percent) you may want to buy new seed, choose a different seed source or variety, or sow the seed more densely next time. If you have allowed your seeds to get hot or wet, their germination rate may be affected.

Moisture: Are my trays drying out during the day?

Underwatering is much more of a concern than overwatering during the germination process. Never let your towel and top layer of soil dry out. However, oversaturating your soil at this stage is not advisable because you can leach important nutrients. Your objective is to keep your soil, and therefore your seed, moist. In the beginning stages of germination, before the seeds have set roots, focus on keeping the top layer moist instead of worrying about soaking the entire tray.

Temperature: Is the temperature where the greens are germinating too hot or too cold?

Extreme heat or cold is often a factor in poor germination. It is easy to obtain good germination rates with temperatures ranging from 55 to 75 degrees F. Due to the variation from variety to variety, referring to your seed packet can be helpful, as this information is usually provided for you.

If you are encountering any problems with the germination of your seeds, don't be discouraged. One advantage of growing a tray of microgreens versus a field of lettuce is your small investment of time, space, and energy. Simply start another tray, change any variables that you suspect are hindering the germination and growth, and see what happens.

2. What if my germinating seeds are sticking to the paper towel when I pull it off?

Waiting for your first seeds to germinate and grow into microgreens can be quite exciting. If curiosity gets the best of you and you begin taking off the paper towel too soon, simply stop and lay it back down. Feel free to peek at your seeds' progress without completely removing the paper towel. You will know that you have taken it off prematurely if most of the germinating seeds and their fuzzy roots are sticking to the towel as you pull it from the soil. Give the seeds another day, checking in the corner to see if they have rooted. A good sign to watch for is the paper towel lifting off the soil. This shows that the seedlings are pushing up the towel and are ready to see the light and open their first leaves. If you wait too long to remove the towel, your seedlings will be at a great disadvantage. They will become tall and weedy, making them more susceptible to rotting and matting. Getting your timing down may take a couple of cycles, but it will soon become second nature.

3. What if I see mold when pulling up my towel?

You may notice a white fuzz around the roots of your seedlings depending on when you remove your towel. It is easy to mistake this for mold. Rest assured it is part of the natural process of germination and growth. Once the tray is watered, the white fuzz will disappear. However, in poor conditions, mold can occur. If you are experiencing cold, dank, damp weather for long periods of time, your germinating seeds will suffer. You will notice a distinct difference between the white fuzzy roots and the mold. While the fuzz is light and surrounds the root area, you may notice the darker mold covering bare soil or surrounding the seeds. Warm weather crops such as basil and cilantro will be more susceptible to mold. Crops that need a longer germination period and have to withstand the previously named conditions will also be vulnerable. Control your environment to avoid the occurrence of mold. While germinating, use heat mats if necessary or move your greens to a warmer area. Once you spot mold in the tray, uncover your seeds, water them lightly, and provide an environment with more light and air circulation.

4. What if the seeds come up thickly in some and sparsely in others?

There will be times when the tray of microgreens you are growing looks like perfectly even, thick lawn. However, you may occasionally find that your trays have uneven germination and/or growth. There are a few factors at play here. The most obvious is how evenly you are sowing. Slowing down and focusing on spreading the seed evenly is important for even germination. Practice makes perfect.

Another cause of uneven germination and growth could be the quality of the soil or how well it has been mixed. While most of the potting soils that we have tried have shown good results, there have been a couple of types that have seemed to hinder germination of certain seeds. This factor may take some experimentation to resolve, so try different soils to find a good match.

Where the tray is germinating may also play a role. If one part of the tray is in direct sunlight and the other half is in dappled shade, you will notice the corollary germination and growth. When germinating your seeds, find a spot in the shade. Find a place for your growing greens with an even amount of sun and/or rotate the trays if necessary.

Lastly, the seed itself might affect growth. We have noticed with certain batches of seed what we call "wave germination." In this phenomenon, seeds germinate at different times, making for an uneven tray. Uneven germination and growth is usually more of an aesthetic issue than it is a real problem for the home grower.

5. What if my greens start to rot?

There are two main reasons why rot can become a problem. The first is that your greens have too much moisture with too little sunlight. In the heat of the summer we usually water once early in the morning and then again in the evening. This works well when conditions are hot and sunny. However, if a cold front were to move in for a few days, bringing clouds and temperatures in the 60s, watering this same way would quickly result in patches of rot setting into your trays. With cooler, less sunny conditions, watering once in the morning would suffice. Problems with both over- and underwatering are your best access to learning what each crop prefers. You have to take time to notice the conditions your greens thrive in and play with the variables.

Another possible reason for rot in your trays is the quality of water that you are using. Municipal water usually contains chlorine, which plants hate. This is easily remedied with most drinking-water filters. The pH of your water being excessively high or low is another factor to be aware of. Nutrients that would normally be accessible to your greens get locked up and become unavailable. There is a bit of a range of pH preference in the common microgreen varieties, but most like a pH of around 6.5. Testing is easy once you acquire the proper equipment. The pH monitors range from liquid solutions to portable digital units. Keeping your pH in check can solve many problems. Not only will you notice stronger growth and increased yields, but most importantly, you will have healthier plants that are less susceptible to rot and disease.

6. What if my tray of soil gets a crack in it?

You may discover that your soil shifts when trays are moved around. Deep crevasses may occur if the trays aren't carried with even support. Although this may look alarming, your seeds will germinate as usual, and cracks will not affect growth in trays that have already germinated.

7. What if my greens are getting tall and weedy?

Light is always the main factor when you find that your greens are getting weedy. You will notice a distinct difference between healthy, stout greens that are getting adequate light and the tall spindly greens that are reaching for any light that they can find. These greens often become lighter in color as they funnel all of their available energy into seeking out the light. This problem is easily solved by either natural sunlight or grow lights. Make sure you have chosen an area that gets full to partial sun for most of the day. If you find that areas available to you do not have long enough sunny periods, you could choose to move your trays about, following the sun. While moving one or two trays around during the day might not be much of a bother, if you have to move ten trays, this could prove quite time consuming and will increase the chances of dropping trays. If you find yourself in this situation, you may choose to investigate grow lights. Resources for energy-efficient models are available in the back of the book.

8. What if my greens are yellowing and stunted?

Greens become stunted when they are not given enough nutrients to thrive. When growing them in soil, the type of soil is the first thing to look at. Some lesser-quality soils don't have the diversity of nutrients needed to sustain growth. Instead of continuing to grow, you will find that the seedlings simply halt their growth and begin to yellow and eventually rot.

Water pH can also be a contributing problem. See "What if my greens start to rot?" for pH tips.

9. What if the leaves of my greens look burnt?

Sometimes the strength of the sun can cause burning of the leaves. This damage is irreversible and weakens the integrity of the greens. Leaves that have been burnt are less aesthetically appealing, and their longevity after harvest also becomes compromised. Sun damage is easily avoided by relocating your greens to partial shade when the sun is very strong. Avoid watering in the heat of the day, as this can also cause burning. You may find more damage on the edges of your trays because they tend to dry out sooner. In this case, take your time to cut around these greens to salvage at least part of the tray.

10. What if my greens become limp after harvesting?

Because of the delicate nature of microgreens, care must be taken when storing them after harvest. Do not let your harvested greens sit in open air (especially in the heat) for any length of time. When washing your greens, be sure to get them into a cool water wash quickly to keep them fresh and vital. Sloppy storage can also lead to limp greens. Be sure that the container that you are using to store your greens, whether it be bags or a sealable container, is sealed tightly. When treated and stored properly, greens can last up to a week or more in your refrigerator.

RECOMMENDED BOOKS AND RESOURCES

Buy Local

We always recommend checking to see what your local gardening or horticultural store has to offer before looking online and ordering from faraway places. The concept of buying local goes beyond food; supporting your local economy plays an important role in the sustainability of our communities. You will also find that shopkeepers are often very knowledgeable and can answer many of your questions.

Apprenticing

We cannot say enough about the importance of hands-on experience when learning the craft of farming. Opening a textbook on agriculture will only get you so far. Fortunately, there are opportunities all over the world to live and work with experienced farmers. If you have any desire to learn the practical aspects of working with the land, animals, and crops, take this opportunity! There are several extensive networks available to link you with your ideal situation. From season-long commitments to flexible openings, apprenticeships are a fantastic way to deepen your understanding of the land and whatever specific passion you may have or may develop.

www.attra.ncat.org
www.wwoof.org
www.organicvolunteers.org

Community Supported Agriculture

CSAs provide communities and their local farmers a way to come together to form partnerships. Also known as subscription farms, they have been popping up all over the country since the mid '80s. Although there are endless variations on the theme, the basic idea of a CSA is that the farm provides a share of the harvest each week to their shareholders. This usually amounts to a box filled with a variety of whatever is being produced (i.e., vegetables, fruit, dairy, meat, eggs, or bread).

At the beginning of the season, a farmer determines how many shares he or she can produce each week. Families or individuals then pre-buy these shares; pricing structures range from paying for the season's produce in advance to flexible payment plans. This model secures the farm's income at the beginning of the season, ensuring that the community has access to local farm goods.

CSAs allow for people to connect with the source of their food. They also provide a great opportunity for children to learn about where their food comes from. They can see their veggies growing, meet the farm animals, and even pick some strawberries themselves. This gives people a chance to experience their produce through the seasons, finding new ways to cook whatever is in abundance and to anticipate what is coming in the months ahead. It is a wonderful way to support your local farmer and eat seasonally. Look to see if there are any CSAs in your area by checking out www.localharvest.org/csa.

The Pizza Farm

A Living Demonstration

The Pizza Farm was created to educate and entertain "city folk" of all ages about how their food is grown. The Pizza Farm is a "living" demonstration farm that conducts guided tours for schools and tourists, teaching them about agriculture along the way. The Pizza Farm is circular (like a pizza) and is divided into eight pie-shaped "slices," with each "slice" growing or grazing all the ingredients needed to make a farm-fresh pizza. Guests at the Pizza Farm see, touch, and learn about how farmers grow wheat for the crust and tomatoes for the sauce. They also learn about the dairy cows that give milk to make cheese and even the pigs for pepperoni. In a unique and entertaining way, visitors to the Pizza Farm quickly realize they could not enjoy their favorite food without the help of a farmer! For more information, visit www.thepizzafarm.com.

(Information courtesy of www.thepizzafarm.com.)

Books and Magazines

We have found this reading material to be useful and inspiring. Much of it expands on topics that we have touched on in the book.

The Small Farmer's Journal edited by Lynn Miller—Whether you are interested in any aspect of life on the small farm or curious about draft animals, this magazine is a phenomenal resource.

The New Organic Grower by Eliot Coleman—Not only is this book an essential read for anyone interested in growing vegetables, but his annotated bibliography is the best that we have come across.

Four Season Harvest by Eliot Coleman

The Garden Primer by Barbara Damrosch

Soil and Health by Sir Albert Howard

The Rodale Book of Composting by Deborah L. Martin (editor), Grace Gershuny (editor), and Jerry Minnich (editor)

Teaming with Microbes: A Gardener's Guide to the Soil Food Web by Jeff Lowenfels and Wayne Lewis

The Worm Book by Loren Nancarrow and Janet Hogan Taylor

Culture and Horticulture: A Philosophy of Gardening by Wolf-Dieter Storl

The Omnivore's Dilemma by Michael Pollan

Feeding People Is Easy by Colin Tudge

Packaging

If growing for the home, any airtight bag or container will work. If you are growing on a larger scale, finding bulk food-grade bags or clamshells can be useful for keeping your costs down.

Uline, www.uline.com

Grow Lights

There are many different types of energy-efficient models online. A quick online search or visit to your local gardening store will give you all the knowledge that you need.

www.littlegreenhouse.com

Knife Sharpeners

We have found both of these kits to be extremely effective at sharpening knives and scissors. Both are available at www.sharpeningsupplies.com.

DMT Aligner Kit
Lansky Sharpening System

Seed Sources

There are many seed sources at your fingertips. The sources that we have named have given consistent quality, quick shipping, and friendly service. All three offer bulk seed.

Mountain Valley Seeds in Utah: *www.mvseeds.com, (801) 486-0480*

Johnny's Selected Seeds in Maine: *www.johnnyseeds.com, (877) 564-6697*

Kitazawa Seeds in California: *www.kitazawaseed.com, (510) 595-1188*

Soil

Soil can be very expensive and inefficient to ship. Look to see what kind of quality soils you have locally. If you aren't able to get any of the soils that we recommend, try to find one with similar ingredients.

Fox Farm (Ocean Forest Blend, Happy Frog) *www.foxfarmfertilizer.com*

Power Flower *available at www.plantitearth.com*

Vermont Compost *www.vermontcompost.com*

Growing Supplies

For trays, lids, heat mats, and anything else that you might need, check out:

Johnny's Selected Seeds in Maine *www.johnnyseeds.com, (877) 564-6697*

SOURCES

Individual Crops

Amaranth
www.hort.purdue.edu/newcrop/afcm/amaranth.html
http://www.hort.purdue.edu/newcrop/proceedings1990/v1-127.html#HISTORY%20
AND%20TRADITIONAL%20USES

Arugula
www.gourmetsleuth.com/arugula.htm
http://greekfood.about.com/od/herbsspices/p/arugula.htm

Basil
www.herbsociety.org/basil/bhistory.php
http://en.wikipedia.org/wiki/Basil

Beet
http://food.oregonstate.edu/faq/uffva/beet2.html
http://plantanswers.tamu.edu/publications/vegetabletravelers/beets.html

Broccoli
http://food.oregonstate.edu/faq/uffva/broc3.html
http://www.organicfood.com.au/Content_Common/pg-brocolli-facts.seo

Cabbage
http://davesgarden.com/guides/articles/view/753/
www.whfoods.com/genpage.php?tname=foodspice&dbid=19

Celery
http://www.foodreference.com/html/celery-history.html
http://food.oregonstate.edu/faq/uffva/celery3.html

Chard

http://food.oregonstate.edu/faq/uffva/swisschard2.html

http://growingtaste.com/vegetables/schard.shtml

Cilantro

www.soupsong.com/fcilantr.html

http://www.whfoods.com/genpage.php?tname=foodspice&dbid=70

Cress

http://mansfeld.ipk-gatersleben.de/pls/htmldb_pgrc/f?p=185:46:2392652887563286::NO::module,source,akzanz,rehm,akzname,taxid:mf,botnam,0,,Lepidium%20sativum,23709

http://www.hort.purdue.edu/newcrop/1492/neglected.html

Endive

http://food.oregonstate.edu/faq/uffva/endive2.html

www.endive.com/cuisine_nutrition.cfm

Mustard

http://www.whfoods.com/genpage.php?tname=foodspice&dbid=93

Pac Choi, Tokyo Bekana

http://en.wikipedia.org/wiki/Chinese_cabbage

http://www.hungrymonster.com/FoodFacts/Food_Facts.cfm?Phrase_vch=Herbs&fid=5908

Pea

http://gardening.wsu.edu/library/vege006/vege006.htm

Radish

http://food.oregonstate.edu/faq/uffva/radish2.html

http://en.wikipedia.org/wiki/Radish

INDEX

A

Agriculture: Community Supported, 16, 178–179; diversity in, 26, 28; holistic approach to, 29; large-scale, 26¬–27; small-farm model, 16, 26; traditional, 26
Air circulation, 39
Alfalfa meal, 122
Amaranth: 66–68; in Asian Mix, 166; in Microgreen Spring Salad with Carrot Ginger Dressing, 154–156; seed viability of, 38; sources, 186
Apprenticing, 178
Arugula, 69–71; growing time of, 54; in Micro Mix, 166; in Spicy Mix, 167; seed viability of, 38; sources, 186
Asian Mix, 166
Asparagus, Chilled Spears with Ahi Tuna, 144–147

B

Baby greens, 22
Bacon-Wrapped Seared Diver Scallops on Potato and Fennel Salad Topped with Micro Cilantro, 148–151
Basil: 72–74; growing period for, 54; in Buttermilk Panna Cotta with Strawberries and Basil Microgreens, 159–161; sources, 186
Beef, Grilled Tataki, with Crispy Wonton and Asian Microgreen Salad, 138–141
Beet: 75–77; in Roasted Baby

Beets with Beet Microgreens and Goat Cheese Crostini, 156–159; seed viability of, 38; sources, 186
Big Sur Bakery, The, 153–161
Bloodmeal, 122
Bok choy. See Pac choi
Broccoli Tasting, 134–137
Broccoli: 78–80; in Broccoli Tasting, 136–137; in Micro Mix, 166; seed viability of, 38; sources, 186
Burning of leaves, 55, 175
Buttermilk Panna Cotta with Strawberries and Basil Microgreens, 159–161

C

Cabbage, 22, 31, 38, 186; purple, 38, 81–83, 166
Cancer prevention, 31
Carbon to Nitrogen Ratio Chart, 118
Carbon, 118, 119
Carrot-Ginger Dressing, 154–156
Celery: 84–86; seed viability of, 38; sources, 186
Chard: 87–89; in Roasted Baby Beets with Beet Microgreens and Goat Cheese Crostini, 156–159; seed viability of, 38; sources, 187
Chemical fertilizers, 27, 28
Children and microgreens, 21–22
Chive-and-Yogurt Aioli, 148–151

Cilantro: 90–92; in Bacon-Wrapped Seared Diver Scallops on Potato and Fennel Salad Topped with Micro Cilantro, 148–151; seed viability of, 38; sources, 187
Commercial growing, 17–18, 42
Community Supported Agriculture, 16, 178–179
Composting: 18, 57, 116–117; amendments for, 121–122; essential elements for, 117–119; making a compost pile, 119–121; receptacles for, 123–124; sources, 188
Coriander. See Cilantro
Cost of growing microgreens, 18
Cotyledons, 22, 47, 56, 57
Crab meal, 122
Cress: 93–95; seed viability of, 38; sources, 187; in Spicy Mix, 167
Cruciferous vegetables, 31
CSA model. See Community Supported Agriculture
Cucumber Salad, Micro Radish and, 144–147

D

Deetjen's Big Sur Inn, 143–151
Diversity in farming, 26, 28
Drying microgreens, 59–60

E

Earthworms. See Vermiculture
Endive: 96–98; in Micro

Mix, 166; seed viability
of, 38; sources, 187; in
Spring Pea Mix, 167

F
Fans, 43, 59–60
Farming. see Agriculture
Farms, 16, 26–27
Feather meal, 122
Fertilizers, chemical, 27, 28
Fishmeal, 122
Four Season Farm, 26
Franks, Eric, 163–167
Fungicides, 28–29

G
Garden cress. See Cress
Germination: and growing
receptacles, 34; lids for, 41,
48–49; moisture for, 38,
49, 50–51, 54; and pH,
40; and quality of seeds,
36–38; and quality of soil,
35; sunlight for, 53, 54;
temperature for, 38, 41;
troubleshooting, 170–173
Goat Cheese Crostini,
156–159
Grilled Beef Tataki with
Crispy Wonton and
Asian Microgreen
Salad, 138–141
Grow lights, 53, 174, 181

H
Harvesting, 29–30, 42,
56–57
Health. See Nutrition
Heat mats, 41
Holistic approach to
agriculture, 29
Hoses, 39

K
Kelp, 122
Knife sharpeners, 42, 181

L
Leggy growth, 53, 56
Lids for germination, 41, 48–49
Lights. See Grow lights
Lime, 121
Limpness of greens, 175
Liquid seaweed, 122
Local food movement,
16, 30–31, 178

M
Maintenance of greens, 54–55
Meal, 122
Metric Conversion Chart, 130
Micro Basil Oil, 159–161
Micro Mix, 166
Micro Radish and Cucumber
Salad, 144–147
Microgreen Spring Salad
with Carrot Ginger
Dressing, 154–156
Mint, 54
Mold, 34, 38, 50, 172
Mustard: 99–101; seed
viability of, 38; sources,
187; in Spicy Mix, 167

N
Nitrogen, 28, 29, 118, 119
Nutrition, 18–19,
27–31, 188–189

O
Our Favorite Micro Salad, 164

P
Pac choi: 102–104; in Asian
Mix, 166; in Microgreen

Spring Salad with
Carrot Ginger Dressing,
154–156; seed viability
of, 38; sources, 187
Packaging. See Storage
Panna Cotta, Buttermilk,
159–161
Pea: 105–107; in Microgreen
Spring Salad with Carrot
Ginger Dressing, 154–156;
seed viability of, 38; sources,
187; in Spring Pea Mix, 167
Pesticides, 28–29
pH meter, 40
pH, 40, 173, 175
Photosynthesis, 53
Phytonutrients, 18, 28, 31
Pizza Farm, The, 21, 179
Potato and Fennel Salad,
with Seared Diver
Scallops, 148–151
Press, soil, 35
Purple cabbage: 81–83;
seed viability of, 38,
in Micro Mix, 166

R
Radish: 108–110; in Asian Mix,
166; in Cucumber and Micro
Radish Salad, 144–147;
seed viability of, 38; sources,
187; in Spicy Mix, 167;
in Spring Pea Mix, 167
Richardson, Jasmine, 163–167
Rizzolo, Michelle, 153–161
Roasted Baby Beets with Beet
Microgreens and Goat
Cheese Crostini, 156–159
Rot, 34, 39, 40, 173

S
Salad: Asian Microgreen,
with Grilled Beef Tataki,

138–141; Micro Radish and Cucumber, with Ahi Tuna, 144–147; Microgreen Spring, with Carrot Ginger Dressing, 154–156; Mixes, 166–167; Our Favorite Micro, 164; Potato and Fennel, with Seared Diver Scallops, 148–151
Santamaria, Domingo, 143–151
Scale of production, 60–61
Scales, 42, 57
Scallops, Bacon-Wrapped, 148–151
Scissors for harvesting, 42, 56, 181
Seed Viability Chart, 38, 188
Seeds: choosing, 36–38; covering, 47–48; sources, 183; sowing, 46–47; troubleshooting, 170
Selling microgreens, 17–18, 42
Sesame Encrusted Ahi Tuna with Chilled Asparagus Spears Topped with Micro Radish and Cucumber Salad, 144–147
Sharpeners, 42, 181
Sierra Mar Restaurant at the Post Ranch Inn, 133–141
Small farms, 16, 26
Soil press, 35
Soil: choosing, 35; composting, 18; covering seeds with, 48; health of, 28–29; sifting, 48; sources, 183
Sorrel, 54
Spicy Mix, 167
Sprayers, 39
Spring Pea Mix, 167
Sprouts, 22
Storage: containers, 43, 181;

instructions for, 60, 175; and nutrition, 29–30
Stunted growth, 34, 40, 56, 173
Sunlight: and germination, 48, 49, 53–55; troubleshooting, 173, 174, 175

T

Temperature: for germination, 36, 38, 41, 49, 53; and storage of greens, 30; troubleshooting, 171
Tokyo Bekana: 111–113; in Asian Mix, 166; in Microgreen Spring Salad with Carrot Ginger Dressing, 154–156; seed viability of, 38; sources, 187
Towel method: 38, 48, 50–51, 54, 59; troubleshooting, 171, 172
Trays, 34, 46, 174
True Leaf Microgreens, 163–167
True leaf stage, 22, 40, 47, 56
Tuna, Sesame Encrusted Ahi, 144–147

V

Vermiculture, 18, 54, 125–127
von Foerster, Craig, 133–141

W

Warmth. See Temperature
Washing microgreens, 58–60
Water, 40, 173
Watering cans, 39
Watering: of greens, 54–55; methods of, 39; of seeds, 46, 49, 50–51; troubleshooting, 55, 170, 173

Weedy growth, 51, 173
Weighing microgreens, 42, 57
Whole foods movement, 16
Wilting, 55
Wojtowicz, Phil, 153–161
Worms. see Vermiculture

Y

Yellowing, 53, 56, 174–175